What White People
Can Do Next

Also by Emma Dabiri

Twisted: The Tangled History of
Black Hair Culture

What White People Can Do Next

From Allyship to Coalition

Emma Dabiri

HARPER PERENNIAL

NEW YORK • LONDON • TORONTO • SYDNEY • NEW DELHI • AUCKLAND

HARPER PERENNIAL

Originally published in the United Kingdom in 2021 by Allen Lane, an imprint of Penguin Random House UK.

HarperCollins books may be purchased for educational, business, or sales promotional use. For information, please email the Special Markets Department at SPsales@harpercollins.com.

FIRST US EDITION

Library of Congress Cataloging-in-Publication Data has been applied for.

ISBN 978-0-06-311271-1

21 22 23 24 25   LSC   10 9 8 7 6 5 4 3 2 1

Our passion for categorization, life neatly fitted into pegs, has led to an unforeseen, paradoxical distress; confusion, a breakdown of meaning. Those categories which were meant to define and control the world for us have boomeranged us into chaos.

—James Baldwin, *Notes of a Native Son*

There is something open and unending in all of us that cannot be contained by the categories of sociological explanation.

—Jonathan Rutherford

Contents

What White People
Can Do Next

Over the years, I have had countless people ask me for advice on "allyship," but until relatively recently I declined, beyond cursory responses. With most of my work to date, I have felt my creative energy was best placed centering on people of African descent, and I've been fascinated by Black Atlantic cultures for as long as I can remember. The Black Atlantic, a concept coined by Paul Gilroy in 1993, is a lens through which to explore blackness beyond the limits of the nation-state. The term incorporates the United States and the Atlantic coastline of Africa, as well as attending to the existence of Black European cultures that have been traditionally sidelined. For me, shining a light on something powerfully generative yet willfully obscured seemed far more useful and, quite frankly, fulfilling than focusing on "white" people, or instructing them on pointers to better recognize my humanity. Yet there has always been the assumption—generally from people racialized as white—that my interest is in "racism," or indeed the word of the moment, "antiracism." When I returned to Dublin during university holidays as an African Studies undergrad, after telling people what I was studying it wasn't uncommon to be met with an

1

affronted, "Oh what, yeah, so you're real anti-white then?" A baffling response, but one I encountered more frequently than you might imagine. Over the years this changed: the automatic assumption that I was a closet black supremacist declined, but suspected "anti-white" sentiment on my part was replaced with the belief that a degree in African Studies equated to studying antiracism. Recently, I recall having a public discussion in which we touched on Afrofuturism, philosophy, and ancestral veneration and its relationship to African concepts of time, as well as the trajectory between the blues and trap music. I enjoyed it immensely and found the interviewer's questions refreshing. Apparently, not everyone felt the same way. At the end of the event, I was approached by a woman who worked in development somewhere in Africa. She said she enjoyed the conversation but felt it was a wasted opportunity; she wanted us to discuss allyship! My heart sank.

Now, through my experiences of being racialized as black in a homogeneously white society as well as through my studies, I *had* become an inadvertent expert in racism, and had learned that it was impossible to study African history without studying Europe, racism and colonialism, and a good dollop of white supremacy too! I did go on to write my PhD thesis on the construction of racial categories, but that was much later. I find it remarkable that an academic racialized as "white" studying, let's say, English folklore would never be automatically assumed to have an interest in "racism." "White" people have not been overdetermined by their race, which is precisely why we have often witnessed scenes of obscene outrage in those moments when whiteness is pointed out and re-marked upon. Recall the backlash, not to mention the complaints to Ofcom (the UK communications regu-lator), when the Channel 4 newscaster Jon Snow re-marked that he'd "never seen so many white people in one place," while describing a pro-Brexit rally. That outrage hasn't gone away either, and the kickback against the Black Lives Matter protests has asserted itself in numerous ways, most pointedly in the British government's threat to ban the teaching of what they term "critical race studies."

But my reluctance to offer allyship advice was about more than all that. Honestly, the word "ally" itself jarred me; I didn't—I still don't—like it. The power dynamic it reproduces makes me feel icky, and I've seen way too many guides talking about the ally and the "victim." In short, I find a lot of the discourse pat-ronizing, both on a personal level and with regard to the prospective ally. It is not a world-making practice.

Indeed, I see a historic opportunity to reconfigure attitudes and reignite imaginations being squandered by an "antiracist" narrative that inadvertently re-inforces much of what it claims to want to overcome, and that in many ways alienates people who might be otherwise persuaded.

One of the things that allyship fails to address is the

fact that you can continue to view black people as inferior while still being committed to their "protection." When I remembered that many of the nineteenth-century antislavery abolitionists were themselves racists who held deep-seated beliefs about black inferiority, I felt even more uncomfortable with the whole "ally" movement. Where the abolitionists differed most from the racist slaveholders was in their response to how racial "inferiors" should be treated; on the belief in "inferiority" itself they were often in agreement.

In certain ways, today's antiracists are the abolitionists of the twenty-first century. A commitment to allyship with black people doesn't automatically mean you don't think black people are somehow inferior: it means you don't think they should be treated discriminatorily as a result. Moreover, the idea that antiracism is an act of grace that benefits the poor black victim obscures the psychological investment in, as well as the costs of, "whiteness," the losses that are imbibed from its poisoned chalice, *for "white" people too*: "capitalism, patriarchy, and white supremacy have seduced and press-ganged people into servitude."[1]

Naming whiteness is necessary; it is the "invisibility" of white people, who are presented just as "people," the default norm from which everyone else deviates, that is part of its normative power-making. Yet the more you state and claim your "whiteness," *without doing any further work* to unpack what *that means*, the more you become fixed to that articulation of self, the more you become wedded to whiteness. Some of the most racist societies have been ones with pronounced "white identities" that coexist vis-à-vis racialized others.

Unfortunately, much of the present "antiracist" conversation is ahistorical and lacking in this analysis. It is also generally devoid of analysis of class or capitalism, which it seems to have largely replaced with interpretations of interpersonal "privilege." As such, I have very intentionally engaged with texts from earlier generations of intellectuals and activists whose work comes with a different set of priorities, aims that seem both clearer and more collective. The 1971 *Rap on Race* is a public conversation between two of the heavyweight public intellectuals of the time, the illuminating James Baldwin and the (somewhat aggravating) anthropologist Margaret Mead. Baldwin reminds us that one of the persistent "truths" of whiteness is that "all Europeans have a deadly temptation to feel a sense of biological superiority."[2] Whiteness is always there, ever-present, determining who gets a chance and who is denied opportunity. But recently I have been starting to visualize it like a horror-film ghoul: it's looming in the shadows, it's threatening, but we can really activate, energize, and empower it by saying its name three times in the mirror. However, once evoked, what the fuck do we do with it? If we summon it and just leave it at large, free to run rampant and unchecked, it's game over as we're all subsumed by its murderous rampage. Much like the horror-film baddie, we should invoke it only to slay it. Without that second, crucial part, we remain under siege, doing its bidding, in thrall to its promises and lies.

This is one of the numerous reasons I increasingly feel a sense of reluctance talking to, or about, a generic category of "white people." This book is of course called *What White People Can Do Next*. While I wanted to create a concrete, practical resource, the title is also a provocation. Before the book was even written, I had "white" people tweeting me to tell me how offensive the title is. You see, there is still something taboo in addressing "white people," and, despite antiracism becoming more mainstream than ever, there is still a reflex against naming whiteness. Nonetheless, it catches your attention, which is precisely the intention. We have to set whiteness up, to name it, to frame it, in order to disassemble it.

While of course there are parallels and experiential consistencies between people racialized as white, the differences that exist between "white people" in different parts of the world are also vast, before we even get into region, socioeconomic class, beliefs, or political allegiances. I think this diversity represents an opportunity to loosen the death grip of "whiteness," a concept that was invented to flatten these differences in the first place.

Which is what we need, because in 2020, in the grip of the COVID-19 pandemic, the world changed. In the wake of the protests that followed the killing of

George Floyd, the proliferation of allyship guides became overwhelming. My old reservations resurfaced, but I also sensed a genuine commitment from a lot of white people to at least start to address centuries-old wounds that continue to infect the present. In response, I created an online resource called *What White People Can Do Next*. It seemed to resonate far and wide. This book is an expanded version of that.

As we reel through era-defining, world-making events, we find ourselves at the dawn of a civilization ready to be remade anew. Drawing together years of study and my personal experiences, as well as my reflections on a year like no other, I present this book as a proposal to usher in that new world.

Most of us, I'm sure, can sense that we're on the verge of something; whether or not that's teetering on the precipice of disaster, or glimpsing the threshold of a reimagined and just reality, the future feels like it's hanging in the balance. The direction we take is no less than the difference between life and death. To continue on the track we were traveling can only mean death. And we reject that. It is our resistance to death that brought us into the streets chanting "Black LIVES Matter." It is our resistance to death that has seen thousands assembling to protest against environmental desecration. Millions of us feel deeply that change is long overdue unless we are to succumb to death.

The same forces that have a disregard for black life,

for the lives of the indigenous, for the marginalized, for the lives of women, are the same forces who disregard the life of the Earth itself—individuals who see themselves set apart from other people, who imagine themselves disconnected from the natural world over which they shortsightedly assume mastery, who see the destruction and degradation of life as a fair exchange for the tightly policed boundaries of ethnonationalist identities, the pursuit of wealth, or the achievement of billionaire status.

All of this we reject. Out of this refusal, other worlds emerge mirage-like on the horizon. But we cannot assume our protestations thus far will be adequate to birth them. We haven't quite cracked the coordinates. Travel there cannot be taken for granted.

I think we've nailed how to say what we don't want, but we find it much harder to articulate what we *do* want—let alone how to achieve it. The protests and the organizing in the wake of the killing of George Floyd have shown us in no uncertain terms that a great thirst for change exists. But it's not so much that there is too much to do, it's more that we require a new, far more expansive, approach to understanding what we want to achieve and the steps necessary to take us there. As the scholar George Lipsitz cautions, "Good intentions and spontaneity are not adequate in the face of relentlessly oppressive and powerful well-financed military and economic political systems."[3]

Understanding Coalition

The outpourings of solidarity and offerings of support that accompanied the Black Lives Matter protests made many of my peers angry, understandably. There were accusations that, like so much else related to black lives, this was a trend, that the black "solidarity" squares that flooded Instagram were empty, meaningless, performative gestures. I would agree, but I would go even further and ask, Isn't that the substance (or lack thereof) of online activism more generally? As a representational tool, isn't it by its very nature performative? We seem to have replaced *doing anything* with *saying something*, in a space where the word "conversation" has achieved an obscenely inflated importance as a substitute for action.

It's hardly surprising, given that we are obsessed with "representation." Incarcerated in a socially constructed domain of signifiers, isn't the ideal activism produced in such a mirror world hollow, gestural, and performative? I wasn't made particularly angry by the events of 2020, because in terms of racism it was just business as usual. I had already been angry, had spent most of my life angry, at racial injustice, at inequality, at the intentional impoverishment of Africa and the global south, but more latterly angry also at the inconsistencies, contradictions, and hypocrisies that seem to characterize so much online "activism" and, perhaps, the current model of activism itself more generally. Collective goals seem to have been replaced by "visibility." Long gone, it seems, are the organized strikes of the black liberation movements of the 1960s. As Lipsitz notes, there is little evidence of the "parallel institutions" that were built then: the Freedom Schools, the community banks, the community land trusts, the breakfast clubs. Where's the program, the consistent set of demands characterizing and unifying this current moment? Lipsitz continues, "People will be seduced and bribed by thinking that if they're visible, their politics are viable, that as long as they live in an economy of prestige, the image of them acts as a simulacrum of reality." But, he warns, "ethnic studies can do very well, while ethnic people are doing very badly."[4]

There is a lot of directionless anger. The feminist poet and scholar Audre Lorde confides that "sometimes it seems like anger alone keeps me alive; it burns with a bright and undiminished flame"—and oh, the spark of recognition that ignites somewhere inside me at those words, but it's a memory of an emotion rather than the feeling of it. For anger, Lorde continues, "like guilt, is an incomplete form of human knowledge. More useful than hatred, but still limited." Anger may be a necessary stage, but take heed, beloveds: both guilt and anger collude to obstruct coalition building and the identification of affinities and points of shared interest that exist beyond categories that were invented to divide us, invented in order to more effectively oppress us.

There are multiple reasons why I wasn't specifically angry at "white" people's responses to the events of that summer, but one of them is that I have no expectations of "white people." In truth, what the year of the pandemic, more so than any other, has taught me is that I have no expectations of any "racial" group. How could millions of heterogeneous people live up to any one singular expectation of mine?

In the UK we theorize about what "white people" should do in the context of antiracism, when in truth we are often generalizing about our expectations of (upper-)middle-class English white people, and making it universal. (The English elite *do* have a quaint tendency to refer to themselves as "middle class," incidentally, which is self-deprecating, in line with cultural class norms, but more perniciously is also rather useful in making their accomplishments appear more earned, than, you know, the result of their granddaddy being the Earl of Aylesbury, not to mention normalizing what is often obscene privilege.) And let's not forget that lots of white people have different responses to each other, in the same way that black folks also differ in their thinking (shocking, I know!). I think it's imperative to say here that I'm not letting "white" people "off the hook" or failing to "hold them to account"; it's just that while I hear these phrases I don't really know what they mean, or even really what they look like. Who adjudicates the accountability in this instance? The court of Twitter?

Amid all the repetitions in the glut of online advice that has proliferated, there are glaring omissions and, even more worryingly, a reaffirmation of the commitment to racialized thinking. Yes, racism is bad, it asserts, yet the conversation is framed as though there are available outcomes *other* than racism when one assumes "race" as a foundational truth.

This unconscious tendency to double down on the racial categories "black" and "white," making blanket statements about the behaviors, beliefs, actions, and desires of diverse groups of people unified under fictive, generic "races," highlights how many of us still apparently believe that race exists as a natural biological reality. I have serious reservations about popular social movements, however well intentioned, that reinforce a reinvestment in racial categories in this way. "Allyship" being described as a "selfless act" exacerbates the division, assuming a fundamental and immutable separateness between "different" "races," offering charity at the expense of solidarity.

Coalition building, on the other hand, is about identifying shared interests. Through observing movements of the past, we can see that groups far more radical than most of ours today often worked *together* (but in some cases separately) in pursuit of common goals, in contexts that were much more polarized than at the present. In the months before he was killed by the police, Fred Hampton, the charismatic young leader of the Chicago chapter of the Black Panthers, created a Rainbow Coalition, between the Black Panthers, the Puerto Rican Young Lords, and the working-class southern whites of the Young Patriots. The coalition organized around the idea that it was in the best interests of black and other oppressed and minoritized people, together with disenfranchised whites, to organize collectively against racism, police brutality, and the inequalities perpetuated by capitalism.

Remember that this is the historical period in which US segregation was dismantled, so it was particularly dangerous and fraught, yet in contrast to today's culture of cancellation, or at least online pile-ons, triggered by the charge of being "problematic" or "toxic," the Black Panther Party (BPP) had a different approach. Regarding the Young Patriots' use of the Confederate flag, that deeply despicable symbol of the slave-owning South, Hampton had this to say: "If we can use that to organize, if we can use it to turn people, then we need to do it." Without being told to, or being "held accountable," the Patriots renounced the flag themselves out of respect for the Panthers.

There are other rich examples connected to the Panthers. When Huey P. Newton, cofounder of the BPP, was asked what white people could do to support them, he replied that they could form a White Panther Party. The White Panthers, a nonracist group, was set up in 1968, two years after the BPP, by Pun Plamondon, Leni Sinclair, and John Sinclair.

The White Panthers' Ten Point Program was *assertive* in its demands for a better life for all. This is an example of "white" people making demands that would benefit both black and white:

1. We want freedom. We want the power for all people to determine their own destinies.
2. We want justice.

Of course, it is vital to remember while coalition building that we cannot subsume everything under one single struggle, but that is exactly why we need coalitions of *shared* interests. Contrast the demands of the White Panthers above with the almost groveling tone of a lot of allyship today. Unless one is a masochist (which of course some will be), is it not also far more persuasive to be presented with a clear vision of the type of society we want to create because *we all* stand to benefit from it, rather than being chastised to transfer your "privilege" to a "black" person, especially when the steps about how to actually do that are at best vague and nebulous—call out racism, take a pay cut, only support "diverse" brands, all interpersonal, all contained neatly within a neoliberal framework, and all cutely infographical for your socials?

By 1972, Huey Newton himself had shifted the

focus of his political activities from Black Nationalism to "intercommunalism," seeking to unite and empower all disenfranchised groups. The original BP Ten Point Program was adapted to reflect this changing focus—for instance adding a demand for completely free healthcare for all black and oppressed people—although this led to tensions within the party.[5] The BPP became more inclusive in its radical vision. With a new focus on injustices, members began to see more parallels between the struggles of *all* exploited and oppressed people, across lines of race and nation.

In racially diverse contexts, such coalitions are often more destabilizing to the status quo than strictly segregated groups. In South Africa, many activists from the late 1970s and early 1980s have spoken of the fact that the apartheid regime was much more reactionary against, and punitive toward, racially mixed organizations such as the African National Congress (ANC), while maintaining more tolerance toward groups who encouraged separatist lines.[6]

The theorist, poet, and philosopher Fred Moten describes coalition as emerging "out of your recognition that it's fucked up for you, in the same way that we've already recognized that it's fucked up for us."[7] Barbara Fields, a professor of history at Columbia University (and the first African American woman to get tenure at that institution), provides, along with coauthor Adam Rothman, a poignant example, writing about the death of a young woman named Hannah Fizer.

Hannah Fizer was driving to work at a convenience store in Sedalia, Missouri, late on a Saturday night in June [2020] when a police officer pulled her over for running a red light. According to police reports, Fizer was "non-compliant" and threatened to shoot the officer, so the officer shot and killed her.[8]

Hannah, whose coworker describes her as "a beautiful person," had no gun. At this stage it's a depressingly recognizable tale. Here's the part that might come as more of a surprise: Hannah was white.

Fields references a database of police shootings in the United States compiled since 2015, writing that

half of those shot dead by police—and four of every ten who were unarmed—have been white. People in poor neighborhoods are a lot more likely to be killed by police than people in rich neighborhoods. Living for the most part in poor or working-class neighborhoods as well as subject to a racist double-standard, black people suffer disproportionately from police violence. But white skin does not provide immunity.

Fields goes on to insist that

those seeking genuine democracy must fight like hell to convince white Americans that what is good for black people is also good for them. Reining in

18

murderous police, investing in schools rather than prisons, providing universal healthcare (including drug treatment and rehabilitation for addicts in the rural heartlands), raising taxes on the rich, and ending foolish wars are policies that would benefit a solid majority of the American people. Such an agenda could be the basis for a successful political coalition rooted in the real conditions of American life, which were disastrous before the pandemic and are now catastrophic.*

Today's allyship fails to build the necessary coalitions identified by Moten and Fields; it lacks the vision of Hampton. With its reliance on information rather than knowledge, its fetishizing of privilege without any clear means of transferal, as well as the ways in which it actively *reinforces* whiteness, allyship is not only not up to the task, it is in many ways counterproductive. If you, potential ally, are relying solely on that type of material and whatever allyship information you can

---

* This is of course not to say there is no need for more targeted policies as well. While certain initiatives will benefit society more generally, the Runnymede Trust, a UK race-equality think tank, argues that, while policy makers might claim that universal policies equally benefit everyone who is subject to that policy, it's not always the case. There are some universal solutions that seek studiously to avoid race and as such end up ignoring and not tackling inequalities.

cobble together from Google—because, never forget the foundational allyship principles: "Do not expect to be taught or shown," and "Google is your friend"— well, then I have little hope about the outcome of all this, no matter how noble your intentions (moreover, we all know about noble intentions and the building materials that constitute the road to hell).

The internet has often facilitated dissemination of information rather than knowledge; as such, even in cases that aren't quite "fake news," online commentary skews to the reductive. It tells you what to think, rather than teaching you how to think! Professor Angela Davis warns us that

> it is so important not to confuse information with knowledge. In this day and age, we all walk around with these cell phones that give us access to a vast amount of information. But that does not mean as a result that we are educated. Education relies precisely on learning the capacity to formulate questions—what we call critical thinking. Learning how to raise questions not only about the most complicated issues, but about the seemingly simplest issues, is so important.[9]

Armed with snippets of (mis)information— untethered from the radical and reflexive environments they were generated from—social media discourse and the "literature" it generates are often distorted, shrill, and declamatory, quite unlike the expansive thinking of the black intellectuals and grassroots activists whose names we evoke but whose deeper lessons we tend to disregard. Today, those who peddle divisive rhetoric and shallow politics are frequently named the spokespeople of our times. In the words of black liberation scholar Cornel West:

> If you do it in a way that is easily co-opted (*or a way that can be easily manipulated to suit the divide and conquer tactics of the ruling classes*), you will be celebrated while you pose and posture as something you're not [my italics].[10]

I often think about the black feminist scholar bell hooks's proposition:

> For me forgiveness and compassion are always linked: how do we hold people accountable for wrongdoing and yet at the same time remain in touch with their humanity enough to believe in their capacity to be transformed?[11]

On the surface, allyship sounds straightforwardly benign and desirable, but, if we actually consider it, I'm not convinced it is either of those things. The message obscures the rigorous, radical, and expansive vision of movements like the Black Radical Tradition, promoting instead a facsimile that does not stand up to scrutiny and that advocates more for inclusion into a system predicated on inequality rather than the creation of new systems or parallel institutions. Yet even on those terms allyship fails, as the steps through which "inclusion" and transfer of privilege would occur remain amorphous and vague.

> An ally is someone from a non-marginalized group who uses their privilege to advocate for a marginalized group. . . . *They transfer the benefits of their privilege to those who lack it.*[my italics][12]

First of all, this is wildly generic. Who is the "non-marginalized group" and who is the "marginalized"? What criteria are we using to determine these positions? Once this is established—which it rarely is, beyond simple applications of terms like "black" and "white"—other problems emerge. The sentiment is framed as white loss, or at least sacrifice. Many white people are not in possession of enough privilege to transfer its benefits to anyone—and even for those that are, *why* would they—beyond being "nice," or as an act of charity and white saviorism (with its links to white supremacy)—feel like sacrificing anything, particularly in the midst of a global recession? Moreover, *how* would they transfer it?

Are the benefits of the "privilege" we are demanding they transfer merely material benefits extracted through the exploitation of the poor? Of migrants? Of sweatshop laborers? Of the environment? Because the mainstream antiracist conversation is conveniently devoid of any analysis of class or capitalism, this crucial question is left unanswered, and the "transfer of privilege" to "marginalized groups," irrespective of individual circumstances (these transfers always seem to be framed in terms of individuals rather than systems), starts to look like the transfer of resources to people in the global north—who, although members of "marginalized groups," still often have structural privilege over other people with whom they might share racial, but not class, identities. In other words, there's a significant gap in access between an Ivy League graduate who works in private equity and an Amazon delivery person, even when they are both racialized as "black," and both will have structural "privilege" compared to workers from the global south, with patterns of consumption that actively put more pressure on those communities.

In the US context, Angela Davis talks about the emergence of a black middle class and the fact that Obama's presidency is emblematic of the rise of black individuals, not only within politics but also within economic hierarchies. She warns that their existence "is not going to necessarily transform the condition of the majority of Black people."[13] In South Africa there has been the rise of a very powerful and very affluent black sector of the population, a black bourgeoisie if you will. . . . It was assumed that once black people achieved political and economic power, there would be economic freedom for everyone, and we see that that's not necessarily the case.[14]

Let's also consider whiteness's *internal* meanings. W. E. B. Du Bois took pains to point out *a century ago* that whiteness does not just entail "skin privilege" but is also replete with various psychological attachments.[15] Writing in 1995, Kathleen Cleaver identifies the "widespread failure to acknowledge that whiteness conveys internal meanings [for white people's sense of self] at the same time [that] it fulfills anti-black functions"[16] as one of the primary reasons our efforts to eliminate racism continue to fail.

We might abhor it, but if a tenuous and fragile feeling of superiority over black people or other minoritized people is all Donny has, why is he going to give that up? What is being offered in return?

Whiteness leaves its adherents in a state of vulnerability; if somebody else's inferiority is a necessary prerequisite for your own sense of self, you are somewhat trapped, if not doomed. You are also likely to violently protect the boundaries of your racial group. If whiteness is being defined as "not being the other" and the subordination of that other, then a reversal of status is deeply threatening to the person's identity. In contrast to much of today's antiracism discourse, David Roediger argues that making "*whiteness*, rather than simply *white racism*, the focus of study has had the effect of throwing into sharp relief the impact that the dominant racial identity in the US has had not only on the treatment of racial 'others' but also on the way that whites think of themselves, of power, of pleasure, and of gender." [my italics][17]

The lack of any coherent or compelling argument as to why "white" people might want to come on board stems, partially, from a lack of theory in these conversations but also from an atomized approach to issues. For those who do want to become "allies," there is the repeated admonishment that they can "never understand." Fair enough, I'll probably never fully understand what it feels like to be a Native American who lives on a reservation, and none of us will ever truly understand what it felt like to be an actual antebellum slave (although their descendants may well have inherited the epigenetic trauma)—but does that need to be stated again and again? Here once more it can feel like one of those online activist slogans that is more concerned with posturing, silencing, and retribution than meaningful outcomes.

What we do require here is an understanding, not so much of an intersectionality of identities, but an intersectionality of *issues*. Linking our struggles together is the work of coalition building, a vision wherein many people can see their interests identified and come together for a common good. We can start to tell new stories, rather than fall back along fault lines that were designed to divide us in order to better exploit us. While radical Black British activists of the 1970s organized along Marxist and anti-imperialist lines, and as such could identify points of solidarity with other groups such as Bangladeshis and the Irish, many of today's online commentators/"activists"/influencers (the definitions are as amorphous as the aims) rely more heavily on racial-identity politics,* and points of solidarity with other identities are often dismissed. In terms of building mass movements, this might be viewed as a tactical error, but perhaps mass movements are not the aim; nonetheless, it's a missed opportunity. The writer Shafi Musaddique describes one overlooked, but potentially ripe, ground for cultivation:

> If our experiences drive our understanding of identity, then one unexplored notion is that Bangladeshis at times feel perhaps ironically close to a white working-class person in the north. Compare the upbringing: low-income manual labour, the invisibility in political and cultural life. Suddenly, we're not so

---

* Identity politics is often dismissed by the right wing and racists. My critique of it comes from an entirely different place and is expanded upon on pp. 139–43.

different. My most joyous interactions often arise with white, working-class northerners.[18]

Where these affinities exist, they are rarely discussed and are unpopular with forces that thrive on division. Race is one of the most powerful, seductive, and enduring myths of the last four centuries; as a "meme" its success is unrivaled. Whiteness and, indeed, blackness are stories, created, like most stories, to give instruction, to teach a lesson. The concept of a "white race" and a "black race" is not something that exists in nature; on the contrary, it is a socially engineered concept *invented* with a very specific intention in mind. That intention was racism. Until we understand this beginning, there will be no happy ending. Until we face the origins of race, racism will endure. Until we come up with a convincing counternarrative we are unlikely to achieve the antiracist world we claim to desire.

Stop the Denial

First things first. This is the most basic. It's at once the easiest and perhaps simultaneously the most difficult, because I know you've already started denying it. No more. Stop the vehement denial, especially to yourself, that you have racist beliefs. *Race was invented to create racist beliefs*—it goes with the territory.

Of course, racism shows up to varying degrees, but at its most fundamental it is the belief that, on some level, white people are superior to black and racially minoritized people, and that "races" have certain predetermined behaviors.

There are a great many things that I love about Ireland and being Irish, yet I experienced so much racism growing up that I left home as a teenager, and, while I return regularly, I haven't lived there since. From the moment I was born, when the nurse told my mother that you oil rather than wash black babies—so I was oiled but not washed, leading to dirt and grime building up all over my body, until at last one of my mother's friends noticed and listened, appalled, as my mother calmly recounted the midwife's sage advice—it was *game on*; racism permeated my encounters with almost everybody and everything. While there were lots of instances of the explicit racism that everyone in polite society can act appalled about, these weren't isolated incidents; racism was merely the "norm." There were very potent stereotypes that were prevalent in Ireland (as they are in many parts of the world), and it was through the framework of these racist notions about behavior and sexuality that I was viewed. Whether it was from authorities, teachers, "friends," friends' parents, boyfriends, or even family members (my mother was estranged from my racist grandfather, and I don't think having a black baby helped), racism was pervasive. It didn't have to be the explicit use of the N-word, although, believe me, I've been called it more times than I could count; racism was alive in the assumptions people made about me and their subsequent responses to me. As one of very few black people not just in my school or in my neighborhood but in the *whole goddamn country*, I was achingly aware of race, every goddamn minute of every goddamn day. Should I ever forget, even momentarily, I would be swiftly reminded.

I left Ireland when I finished school, and I was by that stage emotionally drained in many ways. I had been intimate with in-your-face racism from the time I was four years old (when we returned to Ireland from the US), and I was exhausted. Today, being a black Irish immigrant in the UK has its peculiarly unique ways of, at times, being *a lot*. Beyond just straightforwardly missing home—the migrants' lament—there's my complicated relationship with home, as well as the assumptions made here about Ireland and being Irish, and on top of all that the assumptions made about being *black and Irish*, which are often wildly inaccurate and weirdly disorienting. In many ways, it is through my experience of living in different countries that I know firsthand that we cannot just theorize about one place and apply our ideas to another. Context matters. It's not about one being better or worse. Both the UK and Ireland conceive of themselves as "naturally" "white" countries, with all that that entails. While the US is distinct in that it was quite literally founded on white supremacy, England and the UK have years of skin in the game, whether it is through the history of colonizing the Americas, where the English really distinguished themselves through creating the architecture of race; the later colonizing of Africa and India in the nineteenth century; or indeed take your pick from the Windrush scandal, Jamaica 50 deportations, the disproportionate effects of COVID-19, the fact that black women are five times more likely to die in childbirth and labor, or just general racialized inequality.

When I was growing up in Ireland, there were fewer institutionalized examples but more individual encounters. I was shocked when I moved to London and discovered that most of the black people I met, at least of my age and younger, didn't have firsthand experience of being called the N-word or any of the many other racist childhood delights I can recall (such as the time when I was about eight years old and a male summer school counselor punched me while calling me a black bastard). Because there had been no black community in Ireland, racism was perhaps less institutionally established there. Yet shocking official references regarding attitudes to "colored" children, usually the children of male African students and young Irish women, in Ireland's mother-and-baby homes and industrial schools show that institutional racism did very much assert itself whenever the opportunity arose. And the recent fatal police shooting of George Nkencho, a young, mentally ill Irish citizen of Nigerian descent, sets a worrying precedent. Going home in recent years I have observed the heavy policing of events attended by young black people. It's shocking to behold; this type of policing is just not something I ever would have seen growing up, before there was a significant black population in Ireland. Moreover, the online discourse from too many "white" Irish people justifying why George Nkencho deserved to die, the lurid exaggerations of the events surrounding his death, the claims he had x number of convictions (he had none, not that he would have deserved to be gunned down if he had), and the reliance on racist tropes to describe both George and "black" people more generally demonstrate that the virulently racist attitudes that abounded when I was growing up have certainly not gone away. Rather, they have seemingly found more opportunities for expression! The inherent criminality certain "white" people ascribe to black people blinds them to the fact that this is a potential threat to their civil liberty too (remember Hannah Fizer): the existence of any police force that might be emboldened by killing with impunity is one that everybody should be robustly resisting.

And here in London, even on an everyday-racism tip, there are regular flash points. When out with my young children, I have white people respond with disproportionate rage for minor indiscretions, like not getting out of their way quickly enough, effing and cursing me to high heaven, often in educated tones. It's proved quite shocking to other white people who've observed it, to me not so much. I recognize it all. What I experience today might have a different texture from the almost unspeakable isolation I experienced when I was growing up, but it has the same origin. Over the years these experiences have taught me many things. One of them is how quickly the facade of colorblindness slips when someone is roused to anger.

You see, throughout my life I've been called the N-word, a "black bitch," etc., etc. enough times not to have any delusions about what we're dealing with; believe me, I'm pretty invested in *wanting things to change*, and I believe that desire is there for many of us. I just don't believe challenging microaggressions is enough, nor is the demand for "inclusion." I don't think the current framing has what it takes to achieve even those inadequate aims. And I certainly don't believe that chastising people about their privilege is a compelling narrative.

Effective movement building demands that we identify *shared goals*, while of course remaining alert to the specifics of racism and how they show up differently in different contexts.

Although we have the freedom to create alternatives, as it stands right here and now, we understand ourselves and others through the prism of race. We've been conditioned to see the world through that lens for centuries. Part of that worldview is the internalization of negative and reductive assumptions associated with blackness and generally positive ones associated with whiteness. So, stop the denial! What would make you immune to centuries of socialization? It's a system we've been born into—over that you have no control. What you *do* have control over is what you do next.

Stop the False Equivalencies

Prejudice is everywhere, but most prejudice hasn't translated into the apparatus of race that, four-hundred-plus years after its debut, continues to determine the relationship between the racial categories "black" and "white." When I was growing up, I remember trying to articulate some of the anti-black racism I was coming up against and frequently being shut down, often by adults who, if they didn't aggressively deny it, might equate the racism with their experiences of having red hair (or something equally trite). What I wasn't equipped to explain to grown men when I was ten years old was that, while I'm sure it was painful, redheads have never been codified into law as a subhuman category, or had a centuries-long propaganda campaign waged against them in order to exploit them and rob them of their resources, to facilitate the enrichment of an oppressor group who kept them in bondage; ya see—same same, but different.

This whataboutery is something that apparently shows up with historical regularity. Returning to the *Rap on Race* (I'm actually obsessed with how hip and '70s that title is) between James Baldwin and Margaret Mead, it is important to point out how painful it is in places. For example, Baldwin is talking about slavery when Mead interjects,

> Wait a minute, my ancestors were hunted through the caves of Scotland and tortured. Should I go back now and have a confrontation with the Catholic Scots . . . My ancestors were hunted through caves before they got here. But I don't think it is particularly relevant.[19]

That's correct, Karen (cheap shot, I'm sorry, it's hard; I couldn't resist the alliteration). You've answered your own question—*it's not relevant*—because the legacy of that historic injustice *is not killing you now.* It is not impoverishing your life or diminishing your opportunities; we are not grappling with its aftermath. This history hasn't condemned you, nor has it cast you in the role of a perennial inferior. That is *not* the inheritance of that history. Whenever she draws these false equivalencies, Baldwin proves, of course, a more than capable foil:

> Lots of groups have prejudicial attitudes; the damage is done when these are shored up by power—I don't really object to whatever the governor of Alabama may think he thinks about me. I really don't care what he thinks about anything. But I do object to him being the governor of Alabama. That's where it tends to be crucial.[20]

40

And therein lies the rub. *Power* is what matters here. It is the wielding of power that transforms prejudiced attitudes into legislated differences between life and death. It is the relationship between "privilege" and "power" that dictates whether the privilege is something that translates into a structural advantage worth trying to remove, or whether fixating on it is a time-wasting exercise incapable of bringing about any substantive change.

I want to add as well that suffering is of course subjective, and that no one has the monopoly on pain. You may not experience racism, but that doesn't mean that you are happy, or that your life is easy. It is not about dismissing another person's experience in order to make the claim that yours is more valid. What interests me is thinking about the ways in which a vast array of oppressions or forms of disadvantage might have a common origin, in order to identify ways of coalition building that can focus on the source of the problem, while remaining mindful of the different textures of our varied but interconnected struggles.

Interrogate Whiteness

In the history of humankind, "white people" are babies. You have only existed since 1661! (To be fair, so have "black people.") The idea that different features, hair textures, or complexions have any intrinsic value or meaning, and that they constitute *racial difference*, did not exist before then.*

The myth of a unified white "race" makes white people, from what are in truth distinct groups, better able to identify common ground with each other and to imagine a kinship and solidarity with others racialized as "white," while at the same time withholding the humanity of racialized others. The ability of whiteness to create fictive kinships where differences

---

* While the notion of racial difference originates in the English colonies in the 1660s, it is in the nineteenth century that this evolved into "scientific racism." Scientific racism established the idea that empirical "scientific" evidence could be used to demonstrate that black people were an entirely distinct species. This further entrenched societal stratification according to assumed racial abilities and intelligence. A key text was *An Essay on the Inequality of Human Races* by Arthur de Gobineau (1853).

might outweigh similarities, or where one "white" group thrives and prospers through the exploitation of another "white" group, all united under the rubric of whiteness, constructs at the same time a zone of exclusion for racialized "others," where in fact less-expected affinities and even cultural resonances might reside.

In truth, this is the work of whiteness, whose invention was to serve that very function. Saying that all "white" people *are the same* irrespective of, say, culture, nationality, location, and class literally does the work of whiteness for it. But despite the continuities of whiteness—the sense of superiority that is embedded in its existence—we cannot disregard the differences that exist. This demands a truthful reckoning with the fact that the particulars of whiteness, as well as the nature of the relationship between black and white, will show up differently in different countries and require the crafting of different responses. I'm surprised that this seemingly self-evident observation remains controversial, although I believe that stems partially from the fact that racism is so routinely denied that, unless it is the full-on Klan-congregating-in-your-garden-burning-a-cross variety, many white people will maintain it doesn't exist at all (tbh, these days there are probably folks denying that the Klan is racist, insisting that it's racist to call them racist). However, given that generally racism doesn't show up like that in the UK, by extension UK residents will claim racism doesn't exist there, dismissing it as "only an American problem."

Ireland's position in all this is interesting, especially given how it informs Irish denials of racism. The history of Ireland, a former colony of the British Empire, has commonalities with that of other colonized countries. However, one of the distinct *differences* is that the Irish came to be racialized as "white" in the Americas, quite unlike the peoples of other subjugated territories. Geographical location is important once again. In order to access the privileges of white supremacy, the millions of Irish who flooded into the US from the 1840s onward distinguished themselves from the black people who had already been there for centuries. When Daniel O'Connell, the famed Irish freedom fighter and committed slavery abolitionist, sought to drum up support from Irish Americans for the antislavery cause, he was mostly met with contempt. O'Connell's radical vision, as noted here by Frederick Douglass, the heroic black American abolitionist, was inspiringly expansive:

I am the friend of liberty in every clime, class and color. My sympathy with distress is not confined within the narrow bounds of my own green island. No—it extends itself to every corner of the earth.[21]

In contrast, Irish Americans generally saw their interests best served by the continuation of slavery; its abolition would create a competitive black labor force that would threaten Irish-American employment interests. Furthermore, it is argued that many Irish Americans were keen to align themselves with a good old-fashioned American institution like chattel slavery. This was part of a PR campaign to combat the nativist sentiments that accused new immigrants of anti-Americanness through support for anti-American causes imagined to be more in line with their foreign interests.

Despite Daniel O'Connell's identification of parallels between the struggles of the Irish and those of enslaved Africans, the concept of "whiteness" worked to foreclose solidarities between the Irish and other oppressed peoples in Ireland itself, where notions of whiteness became well established too. This is illustrated by Eamon de Valera's public lament in 1920 that "Ireland is now the last white nation that is deprived of its liberty," or by the Irish republican Erskine Childers, who passionately felt that self-government was necessary for the Irish, whom he saw as "emphatically on a level with white settlers in locations such as South Africa, Canada, the United States, and Australia . . . not with aboriginal, enslaved or subjugated nonwhite populations."[22] Nonetheless, the investment in whiteness in the American context is not identical to the Irish one. Back in the 1980s, when Ireland seemed almost completely homogeneous, the population very much understood themselves as "white," and it was pretty shitty for those few of us who weren't. But I was recently struck by a conversation I had with a "white" Irish artist. He described growing up in the 1980s in Ireland as a working-class Dubliner and the particular stigmas attached to that. Of course, he "knew" he was "white" in Ireland, but it was when he migrated to the US that he found himself reinvented as a "white guy" in a way that was materially different from his position in Ireland, specifically the new status this identity held: the access to unearned privileges and opportunities at the expense of a subjugated African American population. I think this is key—white skin is certainly a "passport" and is associated with unearned advantage, but its status is not consistent, and it has different meanings in different contexts. It is this that we lose sight of when we conflate the specificities of the US with everywhere else.

My experiences in America mirror his, in a way. The distance I felt from my white Irish friends at home in Ireland became more spatially codified in the US. Each summer I spent there, I entered into a black American world, where I had virtually no encounters with "white" people (and the few I had were mostly uncomfortable). I remember returning to Dublin one September and meeting up with "white" Irish friends who had spent the summer in New York or Boston. Now, although we had been in the same country, we had been in different worlds. I barely recognized their stories. These worlds collided when one summer I went to the States with a group of white Irish school friends (New York and Boston, obvs). In contrast to my summers in Atlanta, where I always ended up extending my stay, this was the only year I cut my trip short. The white bro cultures we ended up in, the expressions of "surprise" (okay, let's call it hostility) from "white" American girls about my relationship with my "white" Irish boyfriend, the unwelcomeness I felt in Irish American enclaves, combined with the ease with which my "white" Irish companions slotted into it all, made me think, "Nah, I'm gonna bounce." That was the only summer I ever spent in America when I couldn't get back to Ireland quick enough.

As Ireland becomes a more racially diverse country (since the late 1990s there has been an increasingly visible black and brown presence), it would do well not to take too many cues from either the US or the UK, and to invest instead in the development of a culturally and geographically specific response to racialization on the island of Ireland. These demographic changes are happening at a time when, globally, the conversation around race has reached a historic moment. The concept of whiteness may be well established, but the institutionalized intergenerational racism hasn't had the same opportunities to take root. Before it does, it's time to create new stories. We need to call (un)happy(ily) ever after on the old one. Otherwise, the hope I nurture for the potential of a future Ireland will be squandered.

* * *

In order to reimagine the future, we have to understand the past. Before 1661, the idea of "white people" as a foundational "truth" did not exist. The
Barbados slave code, officially known as An Act for
the Better Ordering and Governing of Negroes, announced the beginning of a legal system in which
race and racism were codified into law, and is where
our understanding of "White" and "Negro"—as separate and distinct "races"—finds its earliest expression. It went on to next inform the Jamaican slave
code (1684) and, on the mainland of what would become the United States of America, the South Caro-
lina slave code (1695).* The new ideas that were
spreading throughout the English colonial world at
that time continue to shape the power structure that
determines "black" and "white" relations to this day.
Colonial Virginia's slave codes were drawn up shortly
after Barbados's. From 1667, in Virginia there were

* The Maryland law of 1861 reflects the first time in legal
history, in the place that would become the United States,
that we see the use of "white." "It represents the needs of
elites . . . to control large masses of laborers and their desire
to have greater access to women." The law provides that
freeborn English or "white" women who enter into marriage with a slave of African descent do so "to the satisfac-
tion of their lascivious and lustful desires and to the disgrace
not only of the English but also of many other Christian
nations" (Battalora, *Birth of a White Nation*, p. 26).

individual laws until the slave code passed in 1705, which went on to be influential throughout the North American colonies and set in motion the chain of events that had us out in the streets in 2020 chanting "Black Lives Matter." Barbados and Virginia, in particular, are fascinating for what they reveal about the English elite's *terror* of solidarities developing between Africans and indentured Europeans. Gather round, kids, I'm gonna tell yis a little story. It's English history hour (the bit they skip in school).

In *The Origin of Capitalism*, Ellen Meiksins Wood argues that a form of agrarian capitalism that began in England had the effect of creating a surplus population.[23] Between 1520 and 1630, England's population more than doubled from 2.3 million to 4.8 million. But what to do with so many pesky paupers? The recently founded American colonies were seen as a way to off-load the English poor, make a ton of money, and undermine the increasingly powerful Spanish. Boom, hat trick!

Now, life for the English poor tended to be a little bit shit in colonial Virginia: harsh, brutal, and short. However, for their masters, the short life span of the easy-to-replace workers was a convenient byproduct of cruelty. Indeed survival, and completed terms of indenture, actually posed a *problem* for those who governed, increasing competition for large landholders as newly freed tenants sought their own fortunes in tobacco. To address the problem of these upstarts, a law was enacted in 1670 barring anyone other than land-owners and keepers of homes from voting in elections. At this stage, the number of Africans in the colony was rising to meet the growing demands of Lord Tobacco, a notoriously labor-intensive crop.

These days it seems almost impossible not to interpret the past through the ideological frameworks of the present. But it is important to note that, even in colonial North America, a short period existed before slavery became entrenched, during which there was something of a mutuality between African and European. As shown in the work of Jacqueline Battalora, "There is ample evidence from court records that Europeans and Africans *of the same class* behaved similarly and were treated so by the courts."[24] In the 1660s, the records show many instances of marriage between Europeans and Africans, with a quarter of all children who were born to European female servants having African fathers.[25]

There are also examples of a short-lived legal parity. Battalora cites the case of an African property owner who whipped a white court messenger, something that was soon to become unimaginable. The people who would *become* "white" were at first referenced in law as "English or other Christians." However, as racial lines hardened, the terminology changed. By midcentury they show up as "English and freeborn," and after 1680 they become "white." Differences in features or skin color had little meaning in the early period. This was soon to change. It is much easier to exclude according to phenotype than to nonvisible markers such as "Christian" or "freeborn."

Against this backdrop, the English landlord and governer class was amassing obscene wealth off the brutalized backs of kidnapped Africans and the English poor. Virginia was a pressure cooker.

In 1676 it erupted, when Nathaniel Bacon, an Englishman and bearer of multiple grudges—against both the ruling elite *and* the native peoples, toward whom he harbored a deep antipathy—started a rebellion. Bacon's Rebellion saw a union of "commoners," both African and English, united in the fight against exploitation and unpaid labor, the excesses of the plantation elite, and those governing the colony. With so many aggrieved people in the colony, it didn't prove hard to get recruits. While the rebellion was ultimately unsuccessful, the governors were—in modern parlance—"shook." Their economic interests had been severely threatened by the revolt. Such an outrage should never be allowed to occur again, and this relatively little-known rebellion would have a long-lasting legacy. As unaware of it as most people probably are, we are all aware of its bequest: the promotion of the concept of white people in North America. (Barbados had gotten there first in the Caribbean a few years previously.)

Theodore W. Allen, the author of the seminal *The Invention of the White Race*, writes that the response to the rebellion was the creation of a new social status. This status would become the birthright of all Anglos and all people of (visibly at least) exclusively European ancestry in North America (and ultimately the world). This "white" identity was designed to distinguish "white people" from enslaved Africans, and to consolidate Europeans across class lines, all part of a system of capitalist agriculture based on chattel bond labor.[26] Just as in colonial Barbados, where slave codes were announced following uprisings in which enslaved Africans and indentured Irish servants had united against English landowners, Bacon's Rebellion resulted in the Virginian slave codes of 1705. As Edmund Morgan writes,

> For those with eyes to see, there was an obvious lesson in the rebellion. Resentment of an alien race might be more powerful than resentment of an upper class. Virginians did not immediately grasp it. It would sink in as time went on.[27]

"Whites" would know their place and "Negroes" would bloody well know theirs. The Virginia slave code was integral to creating division between enslaved Africans and European laborers, while facilitating a fictive kinship between European elites and European workers.

This new status of "white" was a powerful tool for pacifying discontented and impoverished Europeans in the seventeenth century. Indeed, the sense of superiority encoded into whiteness remains a very effective ruse to distract "white people" from the oppression many of them experience keenly: the pressure of financial precariousness, the unaffordability of a home, the erosion of healthcare and education, or any of the other countless deprivations endured while trying to "make a living" in a world that has become increasingly unlivable. The myth of a white race as a biological reality was a (remarkably effective) technique designed to convince "whites" that they are deservedly advantaged compared to racial "others." Yet in the many instances where this is the case—because as a white person your "race" *isn't* one of the impediments to your achieving the good life—the game is still rigged: unless they are part of a particular social class, many are still set up to lose, with little comfort beyond the belief that "at least I'm not black!"

Jacqueline Battalora reminds us that a "social construct like 'white people,' and the idea of there being various human 'races' that it helps maintain, requires an adaptive and ongoing process of production, reproduction, and institutionalization if it is to be rendered common knowledge." There are numerous examples of working-class white people maintaining the reinvestment in whiteness to gatekeep certain job opportunities, a phenomenon we see repeating itself from the Irish Americans in New York in the nineteenth century to the Polish Americans in the factories of Detroit in the 1960s.

A more equal distribution of wealth would be a panacea for much of this, but "whiteness" takes the heat off wealth-hoarding elites while everyone else fights each other.

My fear is that much of the antiracist literature is an iteration of the same process of maintaining and reaffirming whiteness. Little in the mainstream antiracist narrative focuses on challenging the idea of "white people" itself. Rather, it takes the category as an unassailable truth, with the emphasis placed instead on making white people *nicer*, through a combination of begging, demanding, cajoling, and imploring.

"Whiteness" was a concept popularized by convincing one group of people it would make their lives better, and demonstrating it through the brutal dehumanization of another group. Now all "whites," even those with little power in any other quarter of their lives, had the power of life and death over these "others." This is a "truth" that's had close to five hundred years to really embed itself. The question I pose is this: Does telling "white" people that racial equality means that their lives have to literally get worse ("but thems the breaks") really seem up to the challenge of uprooting this centuries-old pernicious promise?

Over the last fifty years we have seen gains in the recognition of the rights of black people, in law at least. Despite this, the treatment of black people by our institutions—from law enforcement and the judiciary, to education and the health sector (although another grave distinction between the UK and the US is Britain's National Health Service)—and intergenerational wealth gaps as well as access to opportunities show that not as much has changed as some might insist. The enduring belief that white people are more honest, more intelligent, more trustworthy, less predetermined to just do bad shit, is still deeply rooted and remains to be tackled. The achievement of civil rights allowed white people to say, "Ah, but now we have civil rights," the same way some English people love to go on about abolishing slavery, problem solved, or indeed how some Irish people will insist, "But we were slaves too, and look how well we did"— this is *proof* that black disadvantage *must* be inherent!

The icing on the self-congratulatory pat-on-the-back cake was the powerful symbolism of Barack Obama's presidency. America had elected a black president, his wife was a descendant of slaves* . . . living in

---

* In fact, Obama is also the descendant of an enslaved woman via his "white" American mother, whose forebear was allegedly John Punch, the "first official slave in the English colonies" in Virginia, an African indentured servant who ran away but was then captured and sentenced to serve as a slave for the remainder of his life. This episode is understood by many historians to involve one of the first

the White House, ffs! It was official. We were living in the beautiful postracial future of Martin Luther King Jr.'s fateful speech. It wasn't long before the illusion was resolutely shattered. Which is hardly surprising, because, throughout all the posturing, whiteness remained untouched. Despite declaring that we were postracial, we were anything but. In no way had there been any attempt to create a different framework for understanding ourselves or each other outside the parameters of race. Whiteness as a truth and as an unnamed system of knowledge remained unchallenged. White perspectives continued to be seen not as "white perspectives" but as objective truths, while black perspectives continued to be perceived as just that: deviations from the norm. Whiteness was not named and it was certainly not questioned.

In the mainstream antiracist discourse, I observe a tendency to behave as though nothing, or at least very little, has changed over the last fifty or so years. Certainly *not enough* has changed, and in some ways things are *worse*—inequality has skyrocketed, for instance, and we know who often bears the brunt of that—but, at the same time, much *has* changed. For the last few years, a process that is well underway, and which was turbocharged by the killing of George Floyd, is the frequency with which whiteness *is* being named.

---

legal distinctions drawn between Europeans and Africans in the colony.[28]

Increasingly, people racialized as white are aware of the racialized perspective informing their worldview, their thoughts, their actions and behaviors. While that is a form of movement, its results are as yet unclear. I have never seen such a widespread identification of whiteness, yet it does not seem to be accompanied by a necessary understanding of the fictitiousness of the category. Unless the idea of whiteness as a "natural" category is disrupted and replaced with something else, the underpinning belief in superiority enshrined as natural to the category will remain intact. And we'll end up back here over and over again. The best we can then hope for is a continued petitioning to the "kindness" of "charitable" whites who might advocate for those of us who are less fortunate.

Doubling down on the sanctity of racialized categories is *far from radical*, although its proponents, including many who identify as "antiracists," remain enamored with the idea. Investment in the absoluteness of racial categories is in fact a conservative, fearful choice. What would be truly radical would be to sound the death knell for the fiction that white people constitute a *race* and that this race is imbued with any "natural" abilities unavailable to others. The first step is the mainstreaming of knowledge about the invention of "race."

After Bacon's Rebellion, the European laborers who had previously worked alongside, and often intermarried with, Africans became effectively their masters. In the newly racialized world order, people of African descent saw any small rights they might have once enjoyed abruptly stripped away. The newly invented "Negro race" could not give evidence against "white people." These "white" indentured laborers saw the terms of their labor, as well as their human rights, enshrined in contract law, and they could expect due process, a *privilege* that became reserved only for those categorized as *white*.

An antiracist movement that emphasizes the *actions* of individual "white people" with a focus on things like "calling out" everyday racism, or holding a company "to account" for not catering to darker skin tones, perhaps isn't up to the task of defeating a concept that our societies have been deeply invested in for centuries, and that has assumed the "truth" status that whiteness has. The focus on microaggressions and interpersonal slights often occurs at the expense of considering "whiteness" as a pervasive, insidious modus operandi, a particular way of engaging with the world. It is a system that is extractive, oppositional, and binary—a dominant system, one that asserts not just that white people should be dominant over other "races" but that, more fundamentally, sees human life as dominant over all other life forms. This is why it is since European expansion that we have witnessed catastrophic events like the destruction of the Amazon and the extinction of countless forms of wildlife, poached and poisoned into nonexistence by a few centuries of exposure to "whiteness," despite having survived for millennia in symbiotic relationships with indigenous peoples. Whiteness violently interrupted our interconnectedness with ecological systems and nonhuman life. And as much as it was "white" people who imposed this system around the world, it remains a system that has also been imposed on people racialized as "white."

If white people are a relatively modern invention, who were white people before they were white? This is a question that will have different answers depending on where you're from. But, nonetheless, whiteness is an erasure, a generic term that collapses crucial distinctions in order to consolidate capital. I recently came across the word *dùthchas,* an ancient Scottish Gaelic ecological principle of interconnectedness between people, the land, and nonhuman beings. *Dùthchas* speaks to the type of coexistence, interrelationality, and entanglement that we are now, perhaps too late, recognizing the utter necessity of, if we are going to survive. These entanglements would be bulldozed over by "modernity": developments like the logic of the French philosopher René Descartes, with its culture/nature and man/nature dualisms, and the Enlightenment humanism that conceived of the world as composed of discretely bounded entities that could be categorized, known, and dominated by "Man" (Man himself also conceived of as a discretely bounded entity). People with physical features that came to be racialized as "white" had existed for many thousands of years before they became reimagined as "white people." That this reimagining was developed and advanced not long after these philosophical developments is no coincidence; the two are inherently interconnected.

"Blackness," too, can be understood in different ways.* Of course, there is the identitarian positioning, including the biological "race" definition, which seems to be enjoying a particular moment of popularity

---

* One particularly fascinating interpretation of "blackness" emerged in the 1805 Haitian constitution. Whatever you might think of it, it is certainly unique to date. Haiti is of huge historical significance as the location of the only successful slave rebellion to end in the establishment of a new country. The new constitution stated: "All meaning of color among the children of one and the same family . . . being necessarily to cease, the Haytians shall henceforth be known by the generic appellation of blacks." According to Sibylle Fischer in *Modernity Disavowed*, "Disrupting any biologistic or racialist expectations, they make 'black' a mere implication of being Haitian and thus a political rather than a biological category." Not only did the label erase previous racial distinctions between "black" and "white" residents, it attempted to undermine the importance of national, linguistic, and color differences within the non-white population. See https://uniqueatpenn.wordpress.com/2015/12/21/race-and-the-haitian-constitution-of- 1805/#ftn5.

online, in keeping with the global rise of reactionary forms of ethnonationalism. Of much more interest to me is blackness as a system of knowledge. Participation in this knowledge system cannot be assumed by one's identity positioning. There are people who are racialized as "black" who engage with the world through the framework of "whiteness." I'm far more excited by the prospect of blackness as "fugitivity." According to Fred Moten, blackness is something "fugitive . . . an ongoing refusal of standards imposed from elsewhere."[29] In *Stolen Life*, he writes, "Fugitivity . . . is a desire for and a spirit of escape and transgression of the proper and the proposed. It's a desire for the outside, for a playing or being outside, an outlaw edge proper to the now always already improper voice or instrument."[30] In *The Undercommons: Fugitive Planning and Black Study*, Moten and his coauthor Stefano Harney articulate the *right to refuse what has been refused to you.* They call this refusal the "first right," and it is a game-changing kind of refusal, in that it signals the refusal of the choices offered.[31] Rather than try to construct "blackness" according to the same parameters as "whiteness," it is in this refusal that we can "reshape desire, reorient hope, reimagine possibility and do so separate from the fantasies nestled into rights and respectability."[32] To paraphrase the philosopher and 'postactivist' Bayo Akomolafe, "fugitivity" is the radical counterpoint to "inclusivity" within the dominant framework of oppression.

People racialized as "white" should be as keen to escape the concept's pernicious grasp as anybody else. When we critique whiteness, or indeed say "abolish whiteness," it is *not* an attack on individual "white" people (nor is it some sort of call to genocide). On the contrary, it is the call to abolish a concept, an idea, an ideology, one that was unambiguously created to divide people, a tool with which to manipulate the exploited to keep them from acting in their own long-term interests.

Of course, rather than engage with any of this, the liberal mainstreaming of the discourse distracts us with trivia like "diversify your feed" (not a problem per se, but woefully inadequate if it's your major contribution to antiracism), or "check your privilege," or things like whether we capitalize the B in "black" or not. Let me consider this last example for a moment, because it's one that is subtle but egregious. I'm not particularly hung up on language. I'm certainly not invested in an ever-proliferating exhaustive list of terms and phrases designed to salami-slice the endless varieties of experience into infinitesimally atomized identity groups. Language is of course not irrelevant, but the capital B—while coming from a place that understandably is attempting to confer more status on to the word "black"—seeks to reinforce a way of seeing the world that we should be disrupting and unraveling. "White allies" using "Black" with a capital B should at least be aware of the thinkers and activists who have intentionally used lowercase for this purpose. The use of the lowercase also makes me think of the black feminist scholar bell hooks (note the small b and its use for de-emphasis) whose framework of "imperialist white supremacist capitalist patriarchy" has been grossly distorted as the bedrock for much of the online "commentary"—and who decided to uncapitalize her name to focus attention on her ideas rather than her personality. When it comes to race, rather than challenging it, we seem to just be digging deeper down into it, CAPITALIZING it, demanding linguistic incarceration, pinning subjects like butterflies to the lepidopterist's board. Akomolafe talks about blackness as freedom, "a roaming principle" as he calls it, with the power to shift, mutate, adapt, and be responsive. This is fugitivity.

Racial categories were invented to enshrine the idea of white supremacy. They are the product of Eurocentrism and colonialism. To act in ways that reinforce their fixedness rather than undermine them is to continue to operate in the terrain mapped out by white supremacy. So, I reject the capitalization of "black." When, out of a lack of anything more suitable, we are driven to use terms that should be contested—terms that are, in the words of Stuart Hall, "under erasure"—we should be seeking to destabilize them. It's the reason that throughout this book I frequently place quotation marks around "black" and "white," intentionally disrupting the comfort with which we rely on that terminology. It's for this same reason that I flinch when I hear the term "mixed race," that most pernicious of racial classifications. While I completely understand why some people use the phrase to describe themselves (there are few satisfactory alternatives), any argument that *insists* that someone *must* use a term that exists to reinforce the "truth" status of a system that is chaotic, nonsensical, and violent, a term that further perpetuates the idea that race is a biological reality, is really not the neutral, commonsense position it might claim to be.

This racialized ordering of the world is endemic to a system that has inculcated us all with a scarcity mindset, which is a great deal at odds with the abundance that truly exists in the world. Boundaries are policed and guarded, resources jealously competed over. Yet rather than reject the system, we internalize it. But there are other options; here, once more, Moten and Harney's "first refusal," the refusal of the choices that are on offer, comes to mind. Depending on what we prioritize, there *is* more than enough to go around: like love, the more you share it, the more of it there is in the world. But of course there's a li'l something that operates as a major deterrent. It's time to talk about capitalism.

Interrogate Capitalism

Capitalism is "an economic system in which the means of production are privately owned and goods and services are exchanged according to levels of supply and demand in markets";[33] *but it is much more than that.*

Capitalism, like "whiteness," is a pervasive organism. It infiltrates the innermost aspects of human experience and transforms our understanding of the world, our relationships with ourselves, with others, with our very environment. In fact, in many ways race and capitalism are siblings. Race, organized according to the black/white binary in operation today, is, as we have seen, a concept invented in the English Caribbean and American colonies in the 1660s, from where it spread throughout the world. One of the primary motivations behind its invention was to justify the exploitation of one group of people for the material benefit of another as part of a larger system called capitalism, and to prevent the emergence of coalitions that could pose a threat to the consolidation of capital. Exploitation and inequality are the operating logic of capitalism. Within such a system, racism will flourish. While capitalism exists, racism will continue. If it's not racism against black people, it will be against another group. Modernity is built upon these foundations.

Understanding the history of "race," and particularly the creation of the fictitious racial groups "black" and "white," exposes the way in which division and exploitation are in the DNA of the racialized order and is key to the conversations we are having about racial injustice right now. I remain surprised that this context is more often than not missing. Without knowing more about the origins of the systems we have inherited, it is difficult for us to identify the fact that many of our best efforts to overcome them merely reinforce them. The structure itself never changes, just the content.

As the rich get richer, the rest of us will be left in increasingly precarious situations. In the global recession that is upon us, the powerful will double down on their control of state and cultural apparatus. They will be determined to repress, or co-opt, the tremulous expressions of resistance that are gaining volume as the people rise up against death. The issue of co-option is pertinent. Our articulations of dissent too often mirror the parameters of our oppression, reproducing oppressive systems, unwittingly reinforcing them, or attempting to reverse them, or indeed *"diverse"* them, to make them more *"inclusive"* when in truth they need to dissolve. Bayo Akomolafe describes our current system as a replication of the slave ship, complete with the various levels that existed on board. In actual slave ships, the captured Africans were chained in the bottom, in the dark, dank hold, with the European slavers on the top deck, livin' it up in the fresh air. Yet although they were on different levels, and as such had radically different experiences of the ship, they were all still aboard a vessel of destruction. Akomolafe says that *inclusion* today can be understood as access to the top deck of the slave ship. Inclusion is access to power in a system that is ultimately a tool of destruction.

It is not enough to make exploitative systems more "inclusive." Do we want to get on the top deck or do we want to destroy the goddamn ship?

Capitalism is often presented as merely the enhanced and refined logical end point of an ancient history of exchange between humans, when in fact it is the culturally specific result of very particular circumstances. As Ellen Meiksins Wood argues,

the distinctive and dominant characteristic of the capitalist market is not opportunity or choice but, on the contrary, compulsion. Material life and social reproduction in capitalism are universally mediated by the market, so that all individuals must in one way or another enter into market relations in order to gain access to the means of life. This unique system of market-dependence means that the dictates of the capitalist market—its imperatives of competition, accumulation, profit-maximization, and increasing labor-productivity—regulate not only all economic transactions *but social relations in general* [my italics].[34]

One of the first concepts an economics student comes across is that of the "rational actor," whose decisions are informed by a desire to "maximize the self." It is of course insane to develop a theory from a starting point that human beings are entirely unmoved by emotions like, you know, love, lust, or jealousy, and that, in all situations, they will be making decisions not influenced by any of those things. I think it was actually the "rational actor" theory that alerted me to the fact that the "con" in "economics" wasn't incidental. While it's wildly inaccurate to assume that this is the way people are behaving, the logic of "maximizing the self" is a potent idea that underpins much of Western modernity, with its presence keenly felt in the neoliberal norm of constant improvement. Where the rational-actor theory disregards the multiplicity of emotions at play, antiracism discourse also seems not to understand that people are motivated by a whole plethora of emotional impulses. The substantive difference between the two is that antiracism behaves as though people will not act in what is at least presented as their self-interest, that they will make decisions influenced only by altruism, and, if they won't make sacrifices for the racially "less fortunate" of their own accord, that they can be publicly chastised into doing so.

"Improvement" played an important role in the relationship between colonialism and the appropriation of indigenous land* by Europeans, as well as in the relationship between capitalism and the invention of race. "Improvement" in this context refers specifically to the enhancement of land's productivity for profit. Meiksins Wood explains that, "by the seventeenth century, the word 'improver' was firmly fixed in the English language to refer to someone who rendered land *productive* and *profitable*."[35] The word "improvement" was well established by the eighteenth century, by which time it was acquiring the more general meaning we give it today. Nonetheless—and this is key—Meiksins Wood asks us to consider the "implications for a culture where the word for 'making better' is rooted in the word for monetary profit."[36]

By the nineteenth century, improvement was

---

* Some of us have at least a familiarity with the ways in which the English went forth and "liberated" the land, from Ireland, to North America, to Africa and Asia. However, we are often less aware that many these processes were also in operation in England, with the appropriation of previously commonly held land. "Enclosures," transforming common land into the exclusive private property of large landowners, became widespread during the seventeenth century; later, between 1750 and 1850, around four thousand enclosure acts were passed, pushing dispossessed workers into the rapidly expanding cities as wage-laborers.

sometimes used without the connotation of commercial profit, but the idea of profit is key to understanding the early modern period, when the concept of race was being engineered, taught, and codified in law. It is unsurprising that even our attempts at antiracism demonstrate the self-improvement ethos that is rooted in economic theory. Capitalism has colonized the most intimate quarters of human experience.

From colonialism to the current "antiracist" movement, the relationship between the improvement of the self and the "improvement" of the land as a justification of its violent theft from the indigenous population highlights the continuity of capitalist logic. What became the United States was literally built by slave labor on stolen land. From before the nation's inception, stolen Africans and their descendants have worked, tilled, and built up that land. For many "white" Americans, their ancestors had an intimacy with black people that was markedly different from the situation in the UK, where black people—while present in varying (generally relatively small) numbers since at least Roman times—have never been present in the way we see throughout the US (and in Ireland far less so). In the US, the psychosocial dynamic has been fundamentally shaped by proximity to a black population whom whites were entirely dependent on—not only in terms of the economies of the modern world but also in terms of the day-to-day functioning of life, from laborers to skilled experts, to the most intimate of carers. Think of the countless black wet nurses who nourished white infants at their breast, while unable to care for their own babies. I often think of this most tender and human of connections in the context of property and the ownership of black women whose very humanity was denied in law.

W. E. B. Du Bois, the polymath scholar and activist who wrote about what he called "the wages of whiteness," explained that the

> status and privileges conferred on the basis of whiteness provided compensation for exploitative and alienating class relationships . . . that even when white workers were paid a lowly wage, they were "compensated in part by a . . . public and psychological wage."[37]

Meanwhile, the UK, with characteristic sleight of hand, generally outsourced its abuse of black people. Nonetheless, the exploitation of black people and the investment in the belief in white superiority would become an enduring cornerstone of both the economy of Britain and its identity. English superiority over the subjugated and the colonized was the ideological underpinning of the empire. The flow of wealth into the UK from the transatlantic slave trade was a crucial part of the industrial revolution, facilitating the development of industry, building the grandeur of many of the country's cities—places like Bath, Bristol, and Liverpool—and creating the framework for the modern banking system. It also laid the groundwork for colonialism. Those parts of Africa that had been looted for human bodies became the territories that Europeans colonized, once colonialism—the extraction of resources and the opening of new markets, that ongoing and relentless pursuit of capitalism—proved more profitable than the trade in slaves. All of this allowed Britain to consolidate more wealth and power.

I think it's safe to say that any antiracist or allyship initiative that disregards the capitalist imperatives (not to mention the deep psychological attachments that fuel "whiteness"), and that imagines that all of this can be undone by missives about "giving up your privilege," is highly unlikely to enjoy success.

It is crucial to connect the dots between the origins of global capitalism, colonialism, and the invention of race. Doing so highlights the fictitious nature of race, as well as revealing the motivations and incentives behind its creation and upkeep. Boots Riley, the communist filmmaker, discusses the movement from workplace organizing—a real and direct threat to capital (recall it was the threat posed by unions of laborers, enslaved and indentured, that inspired the creation of "race" in the first instance in places like colonial Barbados and Virginia)—to student organizing, which in the second half of the twentieth century came to shape concepts of revolution and societal change. Consider the difference between a labor strike and a student strike: one threatens capital, the other threatens little. Riley notes that, with the coming to prominence of the latter model, demonstrations become the be-all and end-all, people being out in the street and creating a spectacle become all important, and the media is seen as key. Yet, he argues, this is all largely symbolic. When you subtract organizing around the exploitation of labor, what is it that you are actually fighting for? The goal becomes more and more amorphous.

Denounce the
White Savior

From slavery through to colonialism, and on to modern expressions of international "development," from ideas about aid and charity initiatives, to guilty liberal complexes, the White Savior is a consistent and recurring trope. The White Savior is such a lovable figure that it pops up everywhere, from Hollywood, to gap years in Africa, to allyship.

The White Savior can only exist because of the power imbalance generated by white supremacy, so it's paradoxical. The White Savior is embedded in the foundational logic of the construction of the "white race." The framework through which the White Savior (and his mirror image, his inferior "colored" charge) would emerge can again be traced back to philosophy, namely the mind/body, culture/nature dualism of Descartes.

"Through slavery and Jim Crow, lynching and mass incarceration, black people have been relentlessly regarded and treated as animal bodies by white people," as the philosopher Crispin Sartwell puts it.

This is not about black people at all, but about the hallucinatory self-image of people who regard themselves as white: it is an attempt to build and enforce a self-image for white people as being spiritual and intellectual beings, and hence suited to know and to rule, to command themselves and hence others, to manage everyone's lives as one's own mind should rationally control one's body. Every white stereotype of black people, first, is relentlessly animalizing or physicalizing, and second, rests on a devaluation of the physical and an exaltation of the intellectual. The association of non-white people with violence and sexuality, with crime or laziness, and their economic exploitation as physical labor, are all rationalized by this application of basic metaphysical dualisms.

This becomes a worldwide structure of oppression, in which rational Westerners, or "experts" of various sorts, are called upon to control unruly and irrational elements: the classic "white man's burden."[38]

The consequences of this remain pronounced, and there are many contemporary manifestations. The allyship space is an arena in which White Saviorism flourishes. One could say that allyship is, in many ways, today's "on trend" articulation of White Saviorism. Given the relationship between Christianity, improvement, and civilizing missions, it's not hard to see the way much of this is linked to notions of being a "good" person and being *perceived* as a "good person." I see certain "white" people almost trying to out-ally each other online, and I have both witnessed and experienced "white allies" schooling black people about not only how they should respond to but also how they should *feel* about racism. I've seen "white" people wading into online disputes between "black" people and, in their eagerness to perform allyship, grossly misreading situations.

While White Saviors might think they are being "good people," black people do not need charity, benevolence, or indeed guilt. It is unhelpful and patronizing.

Quite aside from the patronizing nature of White Saviorism and its racist origins, it seems a huge tactical error to frame antiracism as a petition to the kindness or better nature of the "good," "selfless" individual. As such, allyship appeals to a desire to help a "victim," constituting a reification of the power imbalance.

Coalition, on the other hand, is about mutuality. It reframes the task as identifying common ground—while attending to the specificities of racism—that all can strive for and that all will benefit from.

According to what I learned from searching it on Google—"our trusted source"—allyship consists of

an active, consistent, and arduous practice of unlearning and re-evaluating, in which a person in a position of privilege and power seeks to operate in solidarity with a marginalized group.[39]

85

So, while the ally is unlikely to be a "good" person yet, there *might* exist, *eventually*, through *improvement*, a future good-person version of themselves who will address and somehow rebalance their "white privilege."

We must not forget, either, that the ally's

> needs are secondary to the people we seek to work with. . . . We are responsible for our self-care and recognize that part of the privilege of our identity is that we have a choice about whether or not to resist oppression.[40]

The above instruction is strong with the stench of martyrdom. Most people who will be activated by a demand to disregard their own needs are those who are aroused (and I use that word very intentionally) by White Savior tropes. As a framework it all focuses far too much on the "good" behavior of individuals. The best we might hope to achieve through this type of approach is the reform of a system that is untenable, reform that can only ever be piecemeal and contingent—a fragile safety, a truce unratified by the silent majority, dependent on the charitable but often fickle and self-serving intentions of liberal sensibilities.

We need to shift the focus away from the "good" individual and their personal privilege, moving the emphasis from focusing on racist actions to challenging racist systems. Individual acts and "microaggressions" are of course symptomatic of more pervasive systems, but excessive discourse around them can obscure, distract, and divert attention away from policies, legislation, and institutions through which rights and civil liberties are being dismantled. It's not about one or the other—they are all part of the same ecosystem—but the emotive immediacy of the personal narrative takes up all the bandwidth.

As Professor Davis warns us, "we have to talk about systemic change. We can't be content with individual actions."[41] One feature of the court of Twitter (the jurisdiction in which the expertise of the personal narrative—although only if it hits the right intersections of oppression—reigns supreme) and the movements that find their genesis in online spaces is a form of self-censorship that I find particularly wearying, a mandate that demands ideological purity from the speaking (and the thinking) of others. Any deviation—real or imagined—results in the threat of excommunication from liberal progressive respectability, or indeed from your own identity group. There is for many a new linguistic timorousness, a fear that obstructs us from meeting and recognizing each other fully. It's also a distraction technique. Instead of organizing to create substantive change, we are squabbling with each other over words. These debates might feel very current, but they were happening before many of us were born. In *A Rap on Race* Baldwin and Mead discussed the same thing in the 1970s. They noted that, instead of focusing on structural change, change occurs at the level of vocabulary. Baldwin and Mead discuss the transition from using "negro," in the 1940s, to using "black," which replaced it during the Black Power movement of the 1960s. They then reference "Chicano" replacing "Mexican," a contemporary development in their time. Mead asks Baldwin if he's learned to say it, to which he replies:

> No, not really. It is absolutely new for me. I don't even know where it came from and I don't even know what it means! I don't know how to use it. I don't know whom to ask. Do you know what I mean? It really is kind of frightening because you don't want to use it. I hate people—hippies, for example—who pick up various black phrases and use them to death and don't know what they're talking about. I never want to be caught in that bag myself. So I have become rather tongue-tied too. I don't know what to say. I don't know what that means.[42]

I'm pretty sure this notion of feeling tongue-tied is one many of us can relate to today.

Demanding obsequious language from anyone deemed as possessing "privilege" (while discussion of class is strangely absent) is not a strong foundation for change. Moreover, we need to move away from thinking about individual "good people" to developing just systems.

Abandon Guilt

Remember, you are not responsible for what your ancestors did. You are, however, responsible for what you do. You are also responsible for uncritically accepting all of the advantages accrued to you by virtue of land grabs, wealth acquisition, and their justification story, "white supremacy." But, as we have seen, you might have been, depending on your class position, in some way made materially precarious because of it, and certainly it has imposed a system on you that you are *compelled* to participate in. I would argue that, even if you are not materially impoverished by it, you are spiritually diminished. A system that "builds" you up by tearing others down, that denies the humanity of others, one that not only requires but valorizes the commodification of social relations, is not one that is equipped for achieving the sense of interconnectedness between ourselves and the world that is a prerequisite of good mental health and contentment.

History is now. We are living it. If we can't accept the past and how it affects wealth and opportunity and knowledge production and value systems, we remain doomed to repeat the same mistakes over and over again. But equally we cannot allow guilt and shame about acknowledging that past to paralyze us in a state of inaction and avoidance. I like the distinction Vron Ware draws between the "hand-wringing, produced by guilt," in contrast to the "hand-holding, produced by nonracial solidarity."[43]

Audre Lorde explains it beautifully:

Guilt . . . is a response to one's own actions or lack of action. If it leads to change then it can be useful, since then it is no longer guilt but the beginning of knowledge. Yet all too often, guilt is just another name for impotence, for defensiveness destructive of communication; it becomes a device to protect ignorance and the continuation of things the way they are, the ultimate protection for changelessness.

She continues:

I have no creative use for guilt, yours or my own. Guilt is only another way of avoiding informed action, of buying time out of the pressing need to make clear choices.[44]

Guilt is counterproductive in many ways. Feeling angry about injustice and not doing anything practical about it because you are paralyzed by guilt or shame is useless, but action motivated primarily to assuage your guilt is self-indulgent, often patronizing and misinformed, even, dare I say, privileged. If the objective is to make you feel less guilty, the action runs the risk of being useless, if not detrimental, to those you claim to want to help.

Not knowing what is the right thing to do or perhaps fear of being shamed can prevent people from contributing in ways that might be beneficial and even necessary. I have been involved in an event where someone who was not black but from another minoritized group and who had particular expertise was reluctant to "take up space" despite the fact they had insight into an industry that would have otherwise been missing. The reason given was that they could not have experienced as much racism as the black speakers, by virtue of which they felt unqualified to speak. This brings us back to the centralizing of victimhood; is expertise, insight, and experience now solely determined by degrees of racism endured? And how do we calculate who has endured the most?

Yet, gentle reminder, dear reader, if you are a white person in an "antiracist" space with people from minoritized groups, it is imperative to not dominate these spaces, to ask yourself, Do you really know what you are talking about? Are you speaking over others with the same expertise? Has a lifelong process of conditioning about your own superiority allowed you to assert yourself and speak over others who are in fact *a lot more qualified* on the particular issue? These are all things that have to be negotiated, and will be influenced by the dynamic of the space. For the love of Black Jesus, make sure you are spending at *least* an equivalent amount of time listening to others as you are speaking. If we are working together in solidarity and with integrity, we should have checks and balances in place to negotiate all of this.

There's also the distinction regarding where these dynamics are playing out. A workplace or community organization should have more scope than the social media spaces where much of this occurs. The nature of social media is such that the performance of *saying something* often trumps *doing anything*; the tendency to police language, to shame and to *say* the right thing, often outweighs more substantive efforts. Because shame is so bound up with others' perceptions of you, and social media opens you up to the judgment of an audience of potentially millions of strangers, these dynamics become turbocharged.

Ultimately, guilt and shame have nothing to offer. As a "white" person, dwelling in either state as a response to racism is self-indulgent and white centered; it will also dictate that you prioritize *making yourself feel better*, rather than bringing about any meaningful change.

Pull People Up on Racism

When it comes to achieving a balance between your actions on the broader level and on a more personal one, tackling other people's expressions of racism falls into the latter. While it's crucial not to overstate it, it is important to remember that action can also occur at the individual level. I have been in untold situations where something racist is said, and, as the only black person present, the responsibility has fallen on me to challenge it—not one of the white people present has said anything. It used to be wildly hurtful, exhausting, and disorienting when none of my "friends" would defend me, especially on the unbearable occasions when they also turned on me, with the accusation that I was making everyone feel uncomfortable by defending myself.

I often wonder: if this is the type of thing that happens in front of me, I can only imagine what I am not privy to. So, when family members, friends, partners, or work colleagues reveal racist beliefs, challenge them and, rather than immediately condemn, discuss it with them. You should have more energy to do this work. For black people, arguing the finer details of our very claim to humanity can get pretty tiring.

While we're here, let's also stop insisting racist jokes are just banter.

I grew up in a culture of bantering and, ngl, I love a caustic riposte. And while in certain ways I resent the current policing of language, there is a distinction. I hate to break it to you, but a "joke" in which the gag is that the person is black isn't a joke, it's just racism disguised as humor. A joke told to a white audience where the punch line is a racist stereotype isn't a joke, again it's just racism; if there is only one black person present, it's also cowardly and it's bullying. Jokes of this nature probably aren't funny for black people (Irish people, pay particular heed here). Even if your black friend has learned to laugh along as a survival technique, it is highly unlikely they find your racism enjoyable; in fact it's probably part of an ongoing onslaught that is continuously chipping away at them. Growing up, I had countless friends use openly racist slurs that they defended as craic (Irish banter culture). On one occasion, I reminded a white friend of a racist slur he had called me—as "a joke"—a few weeks earlier. Through an unusual series of events, he found himself in a room full of black people, so I asked him if he cared to repeat the "joke" again. Funnily enough, for some reason he didn't feel like it. The experience allowed him to understand that he only got away with saying certain things to me because of the whiteness of our environment. I think often white people can't even begin to imagine what it would be like to be the minority (and even when they are, it's not equivalent, as the entire history and power dynamic is so different). Nonetheless, in this instance it was a short, powerful lesson that racist jokes are not universally recognized as funny and that, once you spend time outside entirely white spaces, they become much harder to justify.

Stop Reducing Black People
to One Dimension

Stop believing that black people are inherently bad, are inherently good, are inherently anything. I can't believe I'm writing this, because it feels so painfully obvious, yet the allyship framework can be so infantilizing and patronizing that it is sadly necessary. But here's the thing: like you, black people are *people* with the full range of complexity, contradiction, and emotion that comes with humanity. Until white people are prepared to see us as "innocent" (or indeed as less than saintly, depending on what variety of white perspective we are dealing with), racism is present. While there is a strong narrative of black inherent dishonesty amongst racists, at times I've seen almost an inverse of that in some "antiracist" "allies."

Don't believe in some imagined inherent "goodness" of all black people as a response to your own self-indulgent guilt at racism. I'm not going to say "believe black women" or anything trite like that, because, funnily enough, not all black women think the same way, or indeed agree with each other; so if your mantra is "believe black women" you are gonna get some mixed messages and come away pretty confused. Like all human beings, black people are motivated by the whole range of human emotion, and not all of these motivations will be altruistic. To imagine otherwise is dehumanizing.

As the perennially wise James Baldwin reminds us,

> It is very hard. One's got to disengage one's self from any kind of sentimentality. One's got to try to understand what is really happening in this century. The greatest sentimentality, which both black and white have shared for years, is the notion that black people are somehow different from white people. We are different in some ways but, alas, there is one level on which people are not different, and that's the level on which they are wicked. There again you can say that all men are brothers. We've got to be as clear headed about human beings as possible, because we are still each other's only hope.[45]

In the UK, the British Jamaican intellectual Stuart Hall was alert to these tensions too, writing as early as 1989 that what is at issue here is the recognition of the extraordinary diversity of subjective positions, social experiences and cultural identities which compose the category "black"; that is,

> the recognition that "black" is essentially a politically and culturally *constructed* category, which cannot be grounded in a set of fixed transcultural or transcendental racial categories and which therefore has no guarantees in Nature. What this brings into play

104

is the recognition of the immense diversity and dif-
ferentiation of the historical and cultural experience
of black subjects . . . the passing away of what at one
time seemed to be a necessary fiction. Namely, either
that all black people are good or indeed that all black
people are *the same*. After all, it is one of the predi-
cates of racism that "you can't tell the difference because they all look the same."[46]

Hall recognized that this truth required us to then
conceive a politics that could work with and through
difference. One that was able "to build those forms of
solidarity and identification which make common
struggle and resistance possible, but without suppress-
ing the real heterogeneity of interests and identities."[47] It
is this that remains the challenge today.

Blackness is diverse. I am writing this book from
my perspective, which is no doubt informed by my
being an Irish Nigerian woman who spent her early
years in the US, grew up mostly in Ireland with an
Irish mother who grew up in Trinidad, and has spent
most of her adult life in the UK. My perspective
would be no doubt different had I remained in Atlanta, Georgia, where I spent my early childhood.
And despite the relative geographic proximity of
Dublin and London, they are worlds apart, particularly when it comes to black experiences—so it would
be different again if I'd grown up in London, and yet
different again if I'd grown up in Bristol.

I believe our tendency to flatten differences between America and Britain distorts our understanding of both experiences, and prevents us from attending to the specificities of the situation elsewhere. While there are shared histories in part, we cannot conflate the history of a settler colony, shaped by the aftermath of slavery and accumulated centuries of a white-supremacist black/white binary, with the British history of a seventy-plus years' postwar presence of African Caribbeans (also formerly enslaved) and, more recently, African migrants, who were not enslaved but who came from former colonies to the seat of a faded empire. It's also important to consider the shifts in the Black British population over the last sixty years. Paul Gilroy describes it like this:

> Demographically, the Caribbean population has shrunk and the dominant Black settler populations in Britain now are African people from different places, who arrived here under different conditions. Some, not all, arrived as refugees, some as middle-class people with more access to capital. So that generates a very different Blackness. It is more divided and more open . . . to generic forms of Black politics . . . rather than being rooted in the aftermath of the slave experience.[48]

The term "black," much like "white," flattens very different experiences, agendas, and concerns.

106

While it is true that there might be nothing new under the sun, the black American science-fiction writer Octavia Butler reminds us that *there are other suns!*

Instead of exploring these other suns, "white" audiences often seem obsessed with hearing "black" people talk about racist experiences, which is sort of peculiar when you think about the source of the racism and which only serves to center white people again. Of course, there are some white people who are interested in indigenous African cultures, but they constitute far smaller numbers and don't generally look to those cultures for philosophical insights or think about their having much to contribute to world-making politics. We should learn about non-European cultures not just because it is *nice* or "antiracist" to do so but because we're stuck. What lessons might we learn from cultures with different understandings of subjectivity outside of Enlightenment humanism?

Contrary to the popular belief in "ancient" African "tribes," before colonialism "most Africans moved in and out of multiple identities, defining themselves at one moment as the subject of a particular chief or initiate of a religious society, at yet another moment as a member of a certain professional guild."[49] "The 'ethnic' paradigm thus reconfigured becomes less a matter of restrictive labeling and more a matter of choosing . . . dependent on the particular contexts involved,"[50] and this is before we even get into the more metaphysical aspects of precolonial cultures, before the body is imagined as a discretely bounded entity and the rigid structure of "identity" is imposed. In fact, and this is wiiiild, so I need you to pay particular attention, highlighters at the ready:

> Many of the cherished categories of the intersectional mantra—originally starting with race, class, gender, now including sexuality, nation, religion, age, and disability—are the products of modernist colonial agendas and regimes of epistemic violence, operative through a Western/Euro-American formation through which the notion of discrete identity has emerged.[51]

What if those categories that we believe to be sacrosanct, the identities that white supremacy now penalizes us for inhabiting, the identities which we defend to the grave, are themselves expressions of a specifically Eurocentric understanding of subjectivity?! What then?? What do we do when our most "radical" "solutions" are in fact reinforcing the problems we seek to address? What's next?

Read, Read, Read— and Dance

Now, if you've done your research on allyship, you'll have seen this common instruction referred to earlier:

> Do not expect to be taught or shown. Take it upon yourself to use the tools around you to learn and answer your questions.

And we know that "Google is your friend." I mean, I completely understand "Google is your friend" as a throwaway comment to some dickhead on the internet who is trying to derail conversations about race with inane questions, but as a tenet of allyship it's pretty dire. Reading is my portal to other forms of action, and I urge you to read, read, read too. I don't just mean read "antiracist" books. Black people cannot be reduced to our experiences of white racism; that's whiteness centering itself again.

But if you do want to better understand the interiority of black characters through books, read fiction. The most profound truths about the human condition are expressed there, and some of the greatest works of literature happen to have been written by black people. Two of my favorite authors are James Baldwin (you might have guessed) and Toni Morrison. You can't go wrong with those two. If you are going to read theory (and you should), engage with postcolonial writers—the work of Frantz Fanon and Wole Soyinka were revelatory to me—and read up on the Black Radical Tradition: try people like Angela Davis, Fred Moten, Robin D. G. Kelley, George Lipsitz, and Avery Gordon. (By the way, some of these authors are "white" and their writing is profoundly transformative. It's a sad indictment of where we are at when we are more concerned by the identity of the writer than the substance of what is being said.) Unlike much of the work produced by the burgeoning antiracism industry, this is radical work that challenges the neoliberal framework at the root of our oppression rather than passively reproducing it.

The scholar Cedric Robinson, author of *Black Marxism*, a foundational Black Radical Tradition text, describes the BRT as emerging from a split in the black community. On one side, there were those with "a liberal, bourgeois consciousness packed with capitalist ambitions and individualist intuitions." Their objective was "essentially to gain access to the roles and rewards monopolized by whites." Yet on the other side "there was a radical proletarian consciousness that sought to realize a higher moral standard than the ones embraced by whites and their black imitators."[52] And I think that's something we have to be aware of. Not everyone "calling out" the system wants to create a more just one. There are plenty who merely seek access to the levers of power for themselves.

But there are sources beyond books, too. European Enlightenment thinking privileges distance and judgment over other ways of knowing, so we need to think about using senses beyond the problem-solving level. Vron Ware and Les Back urge us to "strive for a democracy of the senses"—to "think less with our eyes."[53] They describe musical cultures as fertile breeding grounds for antiracist dissidents, exploring the potential of sound to undermine the predominantly visual regimes of whiteness and racism,[54] highlighting the potential of DIY culture to create opportunities for new and surprising affinities.[55] The Black Radical Tradition can be found in black expressive cultures outside the mainstream, where the most profound expressions of freedom are located, in roots reggae, in dub, in jazz, in techno, in house, in hip-hop (and sometimes not in the lyrics but in the sonics). That's one of the sites where the movement is liberatory, where it is *black, as in fugitive.*

Use your imagination, use your creativity, tap into other forms of consciousness. Dance, as Emma Goldman, the nineteenth-century anarchist, urged, for a revolution without dancing is not a revolution worth having.

Redistribute Resources

The right to secure housing or to walk through a shop without getting trailed by security are not privileges. They are rights that belong to every human being. Nonetheless, standards of living and access to opportunities have been stratified along racial lines. This isn't always because your ancestors worked harder; it might be because they were thieves. Even if there's no one in your direct lineage who is a thief, the economies that were built on this stolen wealth benefit white communities all over the world.

But redistribution isn't about PayPaling or Venmoing money to black individuals, especially not when it replaces advocating for and achieving collective goals (and is motivated by "white guilt," reinforcing White Savior power dynamics). While there are both interpersonal and structural steps that can be taken, it is not right to pin it all on decisions at a personal level. Relying as it does on acts of kindness, goodness, and charity toward the *less fortunate*, allyship feels like a favor, and favors can easily be withheld. We need policies, programs, and incentives.

But, of course, lots of white people are poor too. We live in a system of unbridled free-market capitalism. Britain is a country in which public services have been slashed, poverty is entrenched, inequality is off the chart, and, for many, a sense of hopelessness and disenfranchisement prevails. The US is many times worse: Jim Crow, spacial segregation, redlining and its legacy in terms of black home ownership and the obstacles it created in regard to wealth acquisition and intergenerational wealth in black families. We might consider how such an environment plays into the hands of those who benefit from keeping people disenfranchised, or indeed those who might benefit from the mobilization of groups of people—who have had other cornerstones of their identities destroyed by the hollowing out of industry and opportunity—around ethnonationalist notions of whiteness. Stripping humans of meaning in their lives, beyond their racial identity, creates a fertile breeding ground for violent forms of nationalism—state, racial, and ethnic—to grow.

When it comes to elections, it's about voting for representatives committed to addressing inequality rather than those committed to personal enrichment and protecting the status quo. Never forget that race—a powerful and emotive mythology, often emphasized in contexts where people have little else to believe in—exists as a persuasive instrument for mobilizing people to act against their own interests and to keep these types in power. As Kathleen

Cleaver says, Du Bois argued that "by the nineteenth century, white workers prized whiteness to such an extent that instead of joining with black workers with whom they shared common interests, they adopted a white supremacist vision that approved of capitalism and 'ruined democracy.'"[56]

Even if we have our faves in power, what keeps the pressure on our politicians is effective lobbies, grassroots activism, and mass movements. Representation is not an end in itself: the election of a minoritized head of state cannot be taken as evidence of substantive change irrespective of markers such as rising inequalities.

Power operates at different levels. Of course, more immediately, personal decisions have a role to play, and what you can do will look like different things to different people. Sitting with your assumptions about black people and challenging yourself is important, and thinking about biases that exist and the power you might have to counteract them, perhaps in terms of hiring or promoting in a business context, could be for you. Think about the capacity you might have for mentoring or other opportunities that can help against structural disadvantages experienced by individuals. Generate your own list.

However, as the scholar and activist George Lipsitz reminds us, it is pretty hard to have good relations when the structure itself is rigged. One of the issues with "antiracism" being optional and interpersonal is a pattern I've seen emerging. During the antiracist frenzy of the summer of 2020 I had a number of wealthy upper-middle-class white people ask me if there were any antiracist resources I could suggest for them to read or watch. Others enthusiastically told me about demonstrations of allyship they had participated in. And yet, since then, in a number of cases I have seen substantive ways in which these people could have made good on the promises of the summer but which they entirely overlooked. Not because they are "bad" people or because they are "white supremacists," but because talk is cheap! This is not about pointing the finger. One doesn't knowingly determine the circumstances of one's birth. It's not about guilt-tripping anyone for having unearned wealth and privilege, although, if this applies to you, why not truly reflect on what you plan to do with an unfair wealth advantage you have inherited as a result of systemic inequality and racism. Martin Luther King Jr. retells "the parable of the rich man and Lazarus," in which the rich man is in hell not because he is rich, but because he has ignored the impoverished plight of Lazarus, when he could quite easily have helped him.

But the responsibility for this should not be left to the whim of choice. We need more equal societies. Because in the same way that one can inherit wealth, one can also inherit poverty. The fact that people's life opportunities and circumstances are still being determined by recent racist history is not acceptable.

Where wealth disparity falls along race or class lines that are a direct result of the history we've spent the last hundred-something pages discussing, there simply needs to be a fairer distribution of resources. Universal basic income (which was actually being proposed by MLK before he was assassinated*) might be one way of achieving this.

Unlike race, inherited wealth isn't a visible marker of privilege. Yet it is the crux of social mobility. According to *The Economist*, 42 percent of King George V's great-great-grandchildren—who are mostly young adults today—work in the arts and entertainment businesses. Increasingly, artists, actors, designers, models, and writers get that leg up or can afford to pursue artistic careers closed off to others because of inequality. Again, this is not to point the finger at these individuals, but it seems, if we are going to talk about "privilege," this is what privilege actually looks like. A recent *Observer* article by Catherine Bennett considered the relationship between political parties, peers, and slavery: "The Conservative peer and celebrated moat-dredger Douglas Hogg, Viscount Hailsham . . .

---

* In 1968, the Poor People's Campaign was set up by Martin Luther King Jr. and the Southern Christian Leadership Conference. A response to the lack of material improvement for many African Americans despite gains in civil rights, the campaign nevertheless embraced all Americans across racial lines.

descends from Charles McGarel, a merchant compensated £129,464 (which has been estimated at over £100m today) for 2,489 slaves," after the abolition of slavery, when the British government compensated the slave owners for their loss of earnings, *but not the slaves*.[57]

This type of direct link between wealth, power, and influence today and its origins in slavery reminds us that this history is far from over, and makes the case for things like reparations and redistributive policies all the more compelling.

An examination of wealth in the US finds evidence of staggering racial disparities and inequality. While we obsess over things like representation, the wealth of those in the upper-income brackets only increases, and is largely unremarked upon. This is clearly stratified along racial lines, with "low levels of wealth . . . much more prevalent among black and Hispanic households than among white households. . . . 25% of white households are in the lower-income tier, compared with about 50% each of black and Hispanic households." Upper-income families also had seventy-five times the wealth of lower-income families in 2016, compared with twenty-eight times the wealth in 1983.[58] In 2016 the net worth of a typical white family was nearly ten times greater than that of a black family ($17,150).[59] "Gaps in wealth between black and white households reveal the effects of accumulated inequality and discrimination, as well as differences in power and opportunity, that can be traced back to the inception of the United States.

The black-white wealth gap reflects a society that has not and does not afford equality of opportunity to all its citizens," say the American authors of *Examining the Black-White Wealth Gap*, and they go on to identify reforms, such as in the taxation of income from wealth, that would help:

> The income from inheritances, and from wealth more generally, is taxed at an inequitably low rate, especially when compared to earnings. Well-designed taxes on inheritances, reforms to capital income taxation, and even taxes on wealth could be part of the solution. Inheritance or estate taxes in particular could enhance equality of opportunity, especially if revenues were invested in programs that give low-income children a better chance at economic success.[60]

The top rate of the US federal estate and gift taxes and the top UK inheritance tax rate are 40 percent. However, the difference in the thresholds at which you become liable to pay tax are enormous. The UK inheritance tax exclusion amount has been £325,000 since 2009. In comparison, prior to the recent US tax reforms under the Trump administration, an individual's lifetime estate and gift tax exclusion amount was a whopping $5.49 million! Under Trump's gentle tutelage, it doubled to a staggering $11.18 million. It could have been worse: the original Republican tax proposal was for a full abolition of the estate tax.

In the UK, white English people have ten times more wealth than black Africans and Bangladeshis.[61] While this may be the same difference in wealth as can be seen between white and black Americans, when we consider that black Americans have been in the US since before the country's inception, and the current black African and Bangladeshi populations in the UK are mostly from recent twentieth-century migration, we see the disparity in progress between black Americans in the US and black people in the UK. What can be done? In its 2020 report *The Colour of Money*, the Runnymede Trust suggests three options that are relevant when thinking about systemic reforms in the UK context:

> First, the Government could better enforce, and employers and service providers could better comply with, existing equality legislation; second, tax-and-spend policies could do much more to tackle poverty and inequality (i.e. more progressive redistributionist policies); and third, greater support for public services that benefit more disadvantaged groups would be likely to disproportionately benefit ethnic minority groups and others experiencing inequalities (especially women and disabled people).[62]

However, once again it is important to highlight the fact that policies directed at everyone might fail to improve the opportunities for those who most need them, and, *quelle surprise*, this is manifested along racialized lines. The French university Sciences Po, trying partly to increase the numbers of ethnic-minority students, gave priority to applicants from regions and areas with relatively high ethnic-minority populations. But they found that, even in those areas, white French applicants were more likely to benefit.[63]

While many people in precarious positions have had their incomes devastated by the COVID-19 pandemic, we have seen huge gains for the superrich during this period. Meanwhile,

> Boris Johnson's Conservative government has been accused of running a "chumocracy," awarding lucrative contracts and well-paid jobs to people with links to ministers and the governing Conservative Party—claims it denies.[64]

It has been widely noted that the coronavirus test and trace chief in the UK, Dido Harding, happens to be married to a Conservative member of Parliament. And in rushing to build up personal protective equipment (PPE) stocks at the start of the pandemic, "the government awarded 8,600 contracts worth $18 billion ($24 billion) between March and July, most without a competitive tender process."[65]

In the US, even more obscenely vast gains during the pandemic have prompted calls for a windfall tax on super-rich tech titans to help pay for the economic recovery from the pandemic. Senator Bernie Sanders and Minnesota congresswoman Ilhan Omar, both Democrats, have introduced legislation dubbed the "Make Billionaires Pay Act" for a one-off 60% tax on the wealth gains of billionaires between 18 March [2020] and the end of the year to help working Americans cover healthcare costs. Under Sanders' proposal, [Jeff] Bezos would pay a one-time wealth tax of $42.8bn, and [Elon] Musk would pay $27.5bn.[66]

It shouldn't be a hard sell; redistribution of resources is very much in the majority's best interests, especially as we attempt to recover from the effects of a devastating global pandemic.

Recognize This Shit Is Killing You Too

On the most basic level, we have to see our struggles as interconnected because they are, and because *we* are. When we zoom out and look at the bigger picture, we see that most forms of exploitation find their source in the same place. But maybe we need to go further still, to approach things in an entirely different way. Activism proposes solutions from an alert, problem-solving consciousness. But perhaps the promise of a society based on this consciousness is already a broken promise.

We exist in a system that has inequality and exploitation hardwired into it. Not only is it destroying human life, it is poisoning our world. It is also destroying you, even if you are not on the front lines (and I don't know, maybe you are): whether you are or are not, it *is* coming for you too.

When I posted the online resource that inspired this book, a "white" woman commented on this particular point, saying something to the effect of "Yes— this is *so* right, this *is* killing me too, I mean it's just *so* painful for me to see my black brothers and sisters suffering so much."

I address that misinterpretation here because, quite to the contrary, I was shifting the emphasis *away* from this type of pitying (white) savior/(black) victim trope, yet somehow yer wan* was bringing it *back* around to the very thing I hoped my work was undoing. My intention was in the spirit of the profound lesson of Fred Moten, with his reminder: "I don't need your help. I just need you to recognize that this shit is killing you, too, however much more softly, you stupid motherfucker, you know?"[67]

So there you go, that's it; print it out, pin it up, tattoo it on your arm, I don't care. But whatever you do, commit it to memory, take stock of the horror that has been unleashed on black people and is felt particularly keenly by the black poor and precarious—then dispense with your pity and your guilt and let's go . . .

We have spoken about whiteness as a refusal (or inability) to recognize basic human connections, and have established that you must be able to recognize another's humanity in order to fully experience your own. Yet the instruction to you as the ally to subsume your own needs as secondary doesn't exactly correspond with engaging your own humanity fully, either. Ask yourself, What type of movement encourages you to build others up by diminishing yourself? Diminishing yourself is entirely different from acknowledging the racialized advantages you possess—yes,

---

*Dublin colloquialism for "woman." (Sometimes, certain vernacular expressions just work perfectly, so here's a li'l taster of the Dublin variety.)

that acknowledgment needs to happen, but belittling yourself feels like some sort of atonement, and that brings us smack bang back to guilt and retribution! No thank you. Not today, Satan.

Yet in so much of this conversation, outcomes seem to have disappeared, too often replaced by point scoring. Barbara Fields and Adam Rothman are insistent on reminding us that attacking "white privilege" will never build the necessary coalitions. They go further, saying that in fact

> white working people—Hannah Fizer, for example— are not privileged. . . . They are struggling and suffering in the maw of a callous trickle-up society whose obscene levels of inequality the pandemic is likely to increase. The recent decline in life expectancy among white Americans, which the economists Anne Case and Angus Deaton attribute to "deaths of despair," is a case in point. The rhetoric of white privilege mocks the problem, while alienating people who might be persuaded.[68]

Here it feels necessary to add a reminder. Don't get it twisted: the fact that white people experience poverty and pain should not be weaponized to try to undermine black people's specific experiences of racism. But just because white people do not experience racism does not mean that their lives might not be fucking shit, or that we should ignore the fact that they might be motivated to identify the origins of their exploitation in the same places others find theirs.

But our culture doesn't view much holistically. Consider our approach to health: our healthcare professionals tend to look at the place of pain without thinking about how it functions as part of a whole. This is the form much of today's "activism" takes too.

Movements like "men are trash" and variations on it show up in online spaces that are described as activist/feminist/social-justice spaces, but, because in the *actual* off-line world men exist as part of our communities, advancing this narrative and calling it feminism is not only contradictory, it is counterproductive. What happens to men has a big impact on what happens to women. Further marginalizing men, particularly minoritized men who are overpoliced and subject to specific and destructive forms of gendered racism, again doesn't seem like an effective strategy. As I've said, too much online discourse seems less concerned with outcomes, and more with point scoring and vengeance. And, you know what, maybe that has its place. There is a lot of legitimate pain and anger out there that is finding expression. I just don't think this type of activity should be misrepresented as "progressive," as activism, or as feminism.

We might want to consider instead the new opportunities and affinities that are opened up through coming together to fight the environmental crisis. Ecological justice groups like Extinction Rebellion are calling for citizens' assemblies—innovative institutions that can allow people, communities, even entire countries, to make important decisions in ways that may be more just and fairer than party politics. Similar to jury service, members are randomly selected from across the country. The process is designed to ensure that assemblies reflect the population in regard to characteristics like gender, age, ethnicity, education level, and geography. Assembly members hear from experts and those most affected by an issue. Members then come together in small groups with professional facilitators and together work through their differences and draft and vote on recommendations.[69]

Such developments are exciting; they allow people to meet off-line and build the type of momentum that can create mass movements. I think familiarizing yourself with these initiatives might be more beneficial than calling out the exploitative brand that hasn't cast enough "diverse" models. I mean, do both if you must, but certainly don't let the latter distract you from the former.

Universal healthcare, free education, access to decent and affordable housing, safe working conditions, and occupations that provide a sense of fulfillment and meaning are all pretty basic and fundamental concerns, yet, for far too many of us, what are really relatively unambitious requirements have become aspirations we can only dream of. Keeping people in a state of scarcity, or shackled to a scarcity mindset, be-holden to the belief that resources are denied to them because of <insert scapegoat racial group> or "im-migrants" (it is not just white people who are manipu-lated in this way; look at xenophobic attacks on and murders of African immigrants in South Africa, for example) serves to distract people from identifying the real source of their impoverishment: the preda-tory capitalism and wealth hoarding of a tiny elite. Preventing the cultivation of common ground that forges a path across artificially imposed lines becomes a simple task, and divisions along racialized lines are automatically fallen back upon in the same way they have been since the seventeenth century.

Postactivism

Ten years ago, probably even five, my response to racism conformed far more to a "speaking truth to power" framework. Like many concepts that become overused to the point of cliché, there was truth and necessity in the framing of "speaking truth to power." At that stage there were still far fewer potential "rewards" for speaking out, in contrast to the celebrification of "activism" that has emerged over the last few years and has been turbocharged by the events of 2020.

There was then, and still is now, a huge deficit in knowledge about the consequences of colonialism and a lack of understanding of the ways in which the imperial conquest redesigned the world according to its logic. I don't just mean the literal carving up of the world and the dispossession of people from their land, or the murderous appropriation of territory by people who came from Europe and their "white" descendants, creating a new world order that continues to benefit white people in terms of offering a materially "better life" on violently stolen land, from the United States, to Canada, Australia, and South Africa. It's not just the kidnapping of, and centuries of enforced labor for, millions of people of African descent, and it's not just the creation of boundaries throughout the continent, or the invention of nation-states, not only in Africa but across the world. Even the nation-state itself is a product of white supremacy, imperialism, and capitalism. The old role of colonial settlers as a means of disseminating economic compulsions has been taken over by local nation-states, which act as transmission belts for capitalist imperatives and enforce the "laws" of the market.[70]

It *is* all of that, but I am also talking about the colonizing of truth, the redesigning of the fabric of reality. I am talking about the imposition of a way of classifying, measuring, and quantifying the world, including everything from time, to temperature, to distance, to weight. All of these things became calculated and bounded by frameworks that were not only European but often peculiarly English ways of understanding reality. Today's activism responds to the world on these terms, operating on terrain already mapped out by white supremacy, Eurocentric logic, and colonialism. This would be less worrying if it was clearly identified, would not pose so grave a danger if there was awareness that the terms of engagement operate within a framework that we need to dissolve. However, that acknowledgment appears to be entirely absent, and we congratulate ourselves on "speaking truth to power" (often, depressingly, via what we now call "platform capitalism").

We must understand the limitations of identity as a

political force. Stemming from the political movements of the 1960s and 1970s, what later came to be understood as "identity politics" reflected a particular approach to organizing (not to mention subjectivity) that was a *necessary* response to the forms of oppression that continued to be experienced by minoritized peoples.

The phrase "identity politics" was coined in the 1970s by the Combahee River Collective, a group of expansively radical women who were black,* lesbian, feminist, socialist. It was their disillusionment with

---

* In recent history the use of the term "black" for people of African descent replaced terms like "Negro" and "colored" after black Americans popularized it during the Black Power/black liberation movement of the 1960s. As a racial category, "blackness" here was not constructed according to an imagined "racial purity" in the way that "whiteness" was. Unlike whiteness, which was constructed with the purpose of hoarding resources, and as such subscribed to notions of exclusivity and the reinforcement of violently policed boundaries, "Black" was inclusive of people who had other ancestry in addition to African. For instance, Audre Lorde, one of the founding members of the Combahee River Collective, had a "white passing" mother and a white Scottish grandfather, while Margo Okazawa-Rey had a Japanese mother. According to the American Association for the Advancement of Science, the average African American genome is nearly a quarter European. Historically, many members of the black community, from Frederick Douglass to W. E. B. Du Bois,

the liberation movements of the 1960s and 1970s, "as well as experience on the periphery of the white male left, that led to the need to develop a politics that was anti-racist, unlike those of white women, and anti-sexist, unlike those of Black and white men." Nonetheless, the fact that "identity" was being mobilized by socialists oriented them toward collectivist objectives, and they were vocal about the fact that they were doing "political work within [their] own group and *in coalition with* other progressive organizations and movements." In contrast, today's online identity politics, expressed through the neoliberal platform capitalism of social media, appears more concerned with protecting only the interests of those within the boundaries of a heavily policed "in" group and more often than not concerned with individual success and the establishment, and protection, of lucrative personal brands. Yet even beyond the obvious limitations of the current hypercapitalist-hell version of identity politics sketched here, the far more ethical form practiced by earlier activists still relied on coordinates mapped out by the codes of white supremacy. While it was a radical and necessary step at the time, which achieved the impressive task of creating awareness of the realities of people whose experiences had been historically disregarded, identity politics requires

---

Rosa Parks, and Malcolm X, were people with significantly "mixed" ancestry.

a self-reflexive understanding of its own limitations (and in fact the collective stated their commitment to "a continual examination of our politics as they develop through criticism and self-criticism as an essential aspect of our practice"). Ultimately, rigid identities need to dissolve in order to avoid becoming immobilized in the death grip of their creator, white supremacy, interlocked in an infinite standoff of oppositional exchange, a struggle that can never end.

Today "identity" has become "a way to manage difference that colludes with dominant forms of liberal multiculturalism."[71] "Difference" produces new subjects of inquiry, that then *infinitely multiply exclusion in order to promote inclusion.* Difference now precedes and defines identity. It relies on the subject X: insert race/gender/sexuality/class/disability.[72] This atomizes the limitless variety of subjectivity into lists of "knowable" categories that "reduce" in order to acknowledge, flattening the complexity of being into neatly bounded classifications that produce a subject defined by their difference who can be governed and appealed to, not to mention targeted for advertising, accordingly.

It is here that we are stuck. Frankly, there's a huge gap in terms of what comes next. While we need to identify what to do, it's important not to fixate on an end point or a final destination; such thinking is part of the problem. Rather, we should try to understand our lives as a dynamic flowing of positions. This is a very different mindset from being wedded to fixed identities, welded to the positions of a rigid "imperial reality," which supposes it can measure and quantify the whole world.*

This is far from the mainstream conversation, but it shows up in the undercommons, in the fugitive spaces that emerge out of the resistance. What if we reject *all* of the options on offer and create our own terms of engagement?

While I want us to understand the origins of whiteness and to name them, unless we are aware of what it is we are invoking when we do so, we run the risk of inadvertently contributing to race thinking becoming even more fixed and entrenched. We have to at least attempt to imagine outside and beyond the race logic inherited from long-dead elite European men, and conceive other ways of dreaming, living, and being.

In the same way that whiteness and racism morph, and are characteristically adaptive and responsive, capable of absorbing and neutralizing whatever threatens them, so we too have to adapt and evolve our strategies accordingly. Even when I was younger and had to remove myself from a majority white environment in

---

* Shout-out to categorization and measurement when it comes to many advances in science and medicine. My issue is with the insane conceit that you can apply the same logic to the entirety of human *being*, belonging, and emotion.

order to breathe more easily, I always had reservations about any serious movement that was entirely determined by rigorously policed and bounded identity lines. The underpinning framework of black liberation was more inspired by revolutionary socialism and international anti-imperialist solidarity than the debased form of online identity politics we see today. My background studying African philosophies taught me that indigenous African cultures perceived a world animated by movement and flow, and that the obsession with purity, rigid classification, and delineated race/gender/sexuality/class identities was a symptom of "whiteness." If we think about whiteness as a knowledge system, rather than as a racial identity, we see that anyone can adopt it and be conditioned to see the world through its lens. You do not have to be "white" to have internalized the white gaze. The colonial state, which morphed into the "independent" nation-state, and the requisite codification and standardization of "tribal" identities and languages, along with European-style "formal" education, have all imposed the "white gaze." Even in Britain, universal education was only introduced to create a "sober," "industrious," "punctual" labor force to generate more capital for the top dogs. It was a system that soon got Africans, and indeed the rest of the world, up to speed.

And here we are today, products of a system few of us are even aware of. Much is against us. Centuries of conditioning, combined with inequality, oppression, exploitation, and injustice have left us defenselessly malleable to the manipulation of mutual antipathies, whose existence serves so well those who benefit from division. On the other hand, we live in a period where many of us from minoritized groups are for the first time experiencing a reality in which we can vocalize our frustrations en masse—in a society in which we not only can name the ways we have been abused but can, perhaps more importantly, at least on a symbolic level, challenge the power and authority that sanctioned that abuse while marginalizing and excluding us from full participation in our communities.

Yet, despite its benefits in terms of potentially democratizing opportunity, the ways social media frames information, and gamifies division, means that it is the quintessential poisoned chalice. The very nature of social media, particularly platforms like Twitter, *reward outrage*; by amassing followers, likes, and retweets from both the like-minded and the cowed, online commentators remain in "angry" setting. Quite frankly, they will generally not be compensated in the same way for offering better informed or more considered takes. When "activism" is bound up in capital relations, and your Twitter persona is your brand, where is the incentive for the recognition of affinity, of solidarity across once artificially imposed lines? Technology, which promised to liberate us, and which has undeniably contributed to gains for individual women, ethnic minorities, and LGBTQ+ people, is a beast of paradox. While it has brought groups that see themselves as the *same*—on the grounds of appearance, race, gender, or sexual orientation—together, the heavily enforced boundaries of those groups contract, cleaning out the competition, and setting up everybody outside their increasingly narrow definitions as an adversary.

And, lest we forget, every action provokes a reaction. While identities we would consider marginalized have been the sites around which we have coalesced, this movement has not occurred in a vacuum. It is not just minority groups who have organized around identity. We have witnessed the upsurge of "white" identity politics that asserts itself in potent, violent, and powerful ways. In the same way that it has operated since its inception in the seventeenth century in the English settler colonies of Barbados and Virginia, "whiteness" has been mobilized once again to encourage people to act against their self-interest. Certainly, it has taught white people to conceive of themselves as the *same* as a group of people who might exploit them but with whom they share a similar skin complexion, at the same time teaching them to understand themselves as fundamentally different and diametrically opposed to others, with whom they might share common interests yet have a markedly different physical appearance from in terms of hair texture, complexion, or other phenotypical features.

We all have common ground. Literally. We all share

the Earth and, as interconnected beings, are not impervious to or unmarked by each other's suffering, no matter how much we have been conditioned to believe we are. Yet when our struggles—those against inequality and racial injustice, or indeed in pursuit of environmental justice—are atomized, our mutuality becomes obscured. And when there are "devil's advocates," hell-bent on derailing—under the banner of "All Lives Matter"—conversations about the specific nature of racism that black people face, points of mutuality become harder to identify. But we don't all have to look the same to identify common interests and perhaps unexpected affinities, to cultivate kinships that cut across divisions invented to weaken us in order to better exploit us.

I believe the cultivation of common ground, or indeed the reimagining of the commons,* to be one of the overarching missions of our time.

I want something to have fundamentally changed by the time you have finished this book, something that will stop us from having this conversation again ten years, twenty years from now.

---

* "Commons can be understood as natural resources that groups of people (communities, user groups) manage for individual and collective benefit."[73] Materials that life requires such as water, air, the earth itself are part of what constitutes the commons.

Does it help to know that this is not the first time we have been here? The slavery abolitionists of the 1700s and 1800s were in many ways today's antiracist activists. And in 1942, Lillian Smith, a "white" US southerner, compiled a list of "things to do" in a piece entitled "Address to Intelligent White Southerners," a set of instructions for those who felt paralyzed by the situation in the South.[74] Her advice ranged from "self-education"—remember the antiracist reading lists of the summer of 2020—to "entering the world of the Negro"; this is in the era of Jim Crow laws, when segregation was de jure, not just de facto, so people were *legally* segregated, unlike today, but it's not a million miles away from 2020's "diversify your feed."

I hope that this book has equipped you with new ways of thinking that get to the root of the issue: the belief—and continued investment in—the *biological* reality of whiteness (or of "race" for that matter). What is key is to detach yourself from the sense of superiority that is encoded into being racialized as "white." The best way to start that process is to recognize the fictitious nature of the category. I hope this book will encourage you to see connections between things you might not have thought about before, and I really hope it will inspire a sense of mutuality rather than charity. I encourage this not because I am appealing to your better nature. Nor am I asking you to "give up your privilege," and I'm not asking you to "amplify my voice" or any other buzzwords. Instead, I am suggesting that you

147

"give up your own oppression" and that you "listen to your own voice," that little one inside that perhaps you silence because, according to the new gospel of "privilege," only the *most oppressed*—although how that is calculated is arbitrary at best—apparently feel any pain. But why is it that despite all of your "privilege," you still feel overworked, underpaid, exhausted, and quite possibly spiritually bereft? You can console yourself with the fact that on top of all that you are not oppressed by racism, but I would argue that you are hoodwinked by the "whiteness" that tells you that you are superior to black people, as a distraction from all the pernicious effects that "whiteness" wreaks.

I want you to think about who "white" people were before they were white. Who might they be afterward? To assess the conceptual limitations of the framework of liberal "antiracism," and to reaffirm the interconnectivity of the human and the nonhuman.

Maybe it is plants who are our allies. The nature/culture dualism that underpins Western thinking and the conceit that man is superior to the "wild" and is lord and master of the natural world has disrupted awareness of our entanglement with our environment and deprived us of the ability to access other forms of consciousness. David Abram, the American philosopher and ecologist, describes our bodies as "sensitive thresholds rather than as bounded entities."[75] Could plants help us reconfigure it all? The psychedelic evangelist Terence McKenna has argued:

Psychedelics are illegal not because a loving government is concerned that you may jump out of a third
story window. Psychedelics are illegal because they
dissolve opinion structures and culturally laid down
models of behavior and information processing.
They open you up to the possibility that everything
you know is wrong.[76]

We need to do things differently. It can no longer
be business as usual. It is a matter of urgency that we
craft responses to racism that don't themselves reinforce a reinvestment in racial categories as absolute
and unchanging facts of life. We need to expose and
end institutional racism without deeper slippage into
beliefs about racial identity as biological essence.

I think that distinction is often a stumbling block
for people. People *do* have different skin colors and
different hair textures. There *are* cultural norms that
one might find more pronounced in certain groups
than in others, and the descendants of enslaved Africans in the Caribbean and the Americas *have* created
cultures that have seduced the world and that are the
engine of Western popular culture, despite the source
of their innovation being routinely denied. However,
race as the framework through which we understand
all of this is not the only option. It was one that was
decided for us many generations before we were born,
and is continuously reinvested in, because it is a remarkably powerful way of achieving certain agendas

and maintaining a poisonous status quo. Racism continues to affect people emotionally, psychologically, and in terms of both access to and denial of opportunity. It continues to be responsible for the death and diminished life opportunities of more black people than we will ever be able to name. As the most basic starting point we need to acknowledge that before we can move on. And move on we must, because "whiteness" as a system is destructive, not just of racialized others, but of everything that it envelops; and while we're busy trying to survive and to overcome racial oppression, we remain distracted from what is possibly the biggest threat we face—the destruction of our very biosphere.

There are no quick-fix solutions, but don't lose hope; the rejection of pervasive white supremacism is a project that forms part of an overarching "politics of change" that offers us, as Vron Ware says, "a form of politics that does not provide short-term gratification."[77] Don't be discouraged by this; the ongoing nature of this work is part of what makes it all the more urgent. As many of us as possible must embark on the journey. There are many others already well traveled; come, let us find them, our fellow fugitives, redouble their efforts, and together dance under new suns glorious and unknown.

Notes

1. Vron Ware and Les Back, *Out of Whiteness: Color, Politics, and Culture* (Chicago: University of Chicago Press, 2002), p. 149.

2. James Baldwin and Margaret Mead, *A Rap on Race* (Philadelphia: Lippincott, 1971), p. 32.

3. Cornel West and Tricia Rose, "George Lipsitz: The Eminem of Black Studies," in *The Tight Rope*, podcast (2020).

4. Ibid.

5. Joshua Anderson, "A Tension in the Political Thought of Huey P. Newton," *Journal of African American Studies*, 16 (2) (2012), pp. 249–66.

6. Ware and Back, *Out of Whiteness*, p. 140.

7. Stefano Harney and Fred Moten, *The Undercommons: Fugitive Planning and Black Study* (Brooklyn: Autonomedia, 2013), p. 10.

8. Adam Rothman and Barbara Fields, "The Death of Hannah Fizer," *Dissent* (autumn 2020), https://www.dissentmagazine.org/online_articles/the-death-of-hannah-fizer.

9. "Angela Davis in Conversation with Yara Shahidi: 'We're Doing Today What Should Have Started 150 Years Ago,'" *Time* magazine (August 2020), https://time.com/ 5880933/angela-davis-yara-shahidi-blm-activism/.

10. West and Rose, "George Lipsitz."

11. bell hooks, http://www.hartford-hwp.com/archives/ 45a/249.html.

12. Holiday Phillips, "Performative Allyship Is Deadly," https://www.holidayphillips.com/blog/performative -allyship-is-deadly.

13. Angela Y. Davis, *Freedom Is a Constant Struggle: Ferguson, Palestine, and the Foundations of a Movement* (Chicago: Haymarket Books, 2016), p. 39.

14. Ibid., p. 40.

15. See Ware and Back, *Out of Whiteness*, p. 149.

16. Kathleen Neal Cleaver, "The Antidemocratic Power of Whiteness: A Review of David R. Roediger, *The Wages of Whiteness*," *Chicago-Kent Law Review* 70 (3) (1995), pp. 1375–87.

17. See Ware and Back, *Out of Whiteness*, p. 19.

18. Shafi Musaddique, "A Forgotten Community: Bangla- deshis Continue to Be Marginalised in Modern Britain," *Byline Times*, October 27, 2020, https://bylinetimes.com /2020/10/27/bangladeshi-marginalisation-britain/.

19. Baldwin and Mead, *A Rap on Race*, pp. 190–91.

20. Ibid., p. 131.

21. Frederick Douglass, letter to William Lloyd Garrison, September 29, 1845, in Philip Foner (ed.), *The Life and Writings of Frederick Douglass*, Vol. 1 (New York: Inter- national Publishers, 1950), p. 120.

22. G. K. Peatling, "The Whiteness of Ireland Under and After the Union," *Journal of British Studies* 44 (1) (2005), pp. 115–33.

23. Ellen Meiksins Wood, *The Origin of Capitalism: A Longer View* (New York: Monthly Review Press, 2017), p. 152.

24. Jacqueline Battalora, *Birth of a White Nation: The Invention of White People and Its Relevance Today* (self-pub., Strategic, 2013), p. 28.

25. Ibid., p. 7.

26. Ibid., p. 41.

27. Edmund S. Morgan, *American Slavery, American Freedom: The Ordeal of Colonial Virginia* (New York: W. W. Norton, 2003), p. 269.

28. Tom Costa, "Runaway Slaves and Servants in Colonial Virginia," in *Encyclopedia Virginia* (2011) , https://encyclopediavirginia.org/entries/runaway-slaves-and-servants-in-colonial-virginia/.

29. Quoted in David Wallace, "Fred Moten's Radical Critique of the Present," *New Yorker*, April 30, 2018, https://www.newyorker.com/culture/persons-of-interest/fred-motens-radical-critique-of-the-present.

30. Ibid.

31. Harney and Moten, *The Undercommons*, p. 8.

32. Ibid., p. 12.

33. Howard Spodek, *The World's History* (combined edition) (Upper Saddle River, NJ: Prentice Hall, 2006), p. 389.

34. Meiksins Wood, *The Origin of Capitalism*, p. 7.

35. Ibid., p. 106.

36. Ibid.

37. Cleaver, quoting Du Bois (partially), in "The Antidemocratic Power of Whiteness."

38. Crispin Sartwell, "Western Philosophy as White Supremacism," https://thephilosophicalsalon.com/western-phi losophy-as-white-supremacism/.

39. See https://theantioppressionnetwork.com/allyship/

40. Ibid.

41. Davis, *Freedom Is a Constant Struggle*, p. 32.

42. Baldwin and Mead, *A Rap on Race*, p. 129.

43. Ware and Back, *Out of Whiteness*, p. 150.

44. Audre Lorde, *Sister Outsider* (Berkeley: Crossing Press, 2007), p. 130.

45. Baldwin and Mead, *A Rap on Race*, p. 45.

46. Stuart Hall, "New Ethnicities," in Houston A. Baker et al. (eds.), *Black British Cultural Studies: A Reader* (Chicago: University of Chicago Press, 1996), p. 166.

47. Ibid.

48. Sean O'Hagan, interview, "Paul Gilroy: 'I Don't Think We Can Afford the Luxury of Pessimism,'" *Guardian*, November 15, 2020.

49. Eric Hobsbawm and Terence Ranger (eds.), *The Invention of Tradition* (Cambridge: Cambridge University Press, 1983), p. 249.

50. David C. Conrad and Barbara E. Frank (eds.), *Status and Identity in West Africa: Nyamakalaw of Mande* (Bloomington: Indiana University Press, 1995), p. 11–12.

51. Jasbir K. Puar, "'I Would Rather Be a Cyborg Than a Goddess': Becoming-Intersectional in Assemblage Theory" (2012), p. 55, http://jasbirkpuar.com/wp-content/uploads/2018/08/JKP_Cyborg-Goddess.pdf.

52. Cedric Robinson, cited in George Lipsitz, "What Is This Black in the Black Radical Tradition?," in Gaye Theresa Johnson and Alex Lubin (eds.), *Futures of Black Radicalism* (London: Verso, 2017).

53. Ware and Back, *Out of Whiteness*, p. 10.

54. Ibid.

55. Ibid., p. 12.

56. Cleaver, "The Antidemocratic Power of Whiteness."

57. Catherine Bennett, "As Statues of Slave Traders Are Torn Down, Their Heirs Sit Untouched in the Lords," *Observer*, June 14, 2020.

58. See https://www.pewresearch.org/fact-tank/2017/11/01/how-wealth-inequality-has-changed-in-the-u-s-since-the-great-recession-by-race-ethnicity-and-income/.

59. See https://www.brookings.edu/blog/up-front/2020/02/27/examining-the-black-white-wealth-gap.

60. Ibid.

61. Runnymede Trust, *The Colour of Money: How Racial Inequalities Obstruct a Fair and Resilient Economy* (2020), p. 13.

62. Ibid., p. 14.

63. Ibid., p. 16.

64. See https://abcnews.go.com/Business/wireStory/watchdog-slams-uk-secrecy-virus-equipment-contracts-74270996.

65. See https://nbcmontana.com/news/nation-world/watchdog-slams-uk-over-secrecy-in-virus-equipment-contracts.

66. Rupert Neate, "Wealth of US Billionaires Rises by Nearly a Third During Pandemic," *Guardian*, September 17, 2020.

67. Harney and Moten, *The Undercommons*, p. 10.

68. Rothman and Fields, "The Death of Hannah Fizer."

69. See https://extinctionrebellion.uk/go-beyond-politics / citizens-assembly/.

70. Meiksins Wood, *The Origin of Capitalism*.

71. Puar, "'I Would Rather Be a Cyborg,'" p. 53.

72. Ibid., p. 55.

73. Soutrik Basu et al., "Development of the Drought Tolerant Variety Sahbhagi Dhan: Exploring the Concepts Commons and Community Building," *International Journal of the Commons*, 11 (1) (2017), p. 144–170.

74. See Ware and Back, *Out of Whiteness*, p. 152.

75. David Abram, "We Will Dance With Mountains," online course with Bayo Akomolafe.

76. Quoted in David Jay Brown, *The New Science of Psychedelics* (Rochester, VT: Park Street Press, 2013), p. 39.

77. Ware and Back, *Out of Whiteness*, p. 13.

About the Author

Emma Dabiri is the author of *Twisted: The Tangled History of Black Hair Culture*. She is a regular presenter on BBC and contributor for *The Guardian*. She is a teaching fellow in the Africa department at SOAS and a visual sociology PhD researcher at Goldsmiths. Her writing has been published in a number of anthologies, academic journals, and the national press. She lives in London.

ALSO BY EMMA DABIRI

"A fantastically interesting and original book which explores black hair through the prism of history, culture, feminism, and philosophy."

—BERNARDINE EVARISTO,
author of *Girl, Woman, Other*